S0-AUP-871

SHUT UP
AND EAT YOUR SNOWSHOES!

"HIS BEST BOOK SO FAR."
> —*Philadelphia Bulletin*

"One of the funniest and craziest books I have ever read. There isn't a dull chapter in it!" —*Charleston Evening Post*

"The funniest thing to come out of the Far North since Rudolph the Red-Nosed Reindeer." —*Buffalo Courier-Express*

"Jack Douglas has picked up the sputtering torch of American written humor that glowed so brightly and was carried so proudly before the deluge of radio and television doused it into a flickering ember." —*Variety*

Books by Jack Douglas

Benedict Arnold Slept Here: Jack Douglas' Honeymoon Mountain Inn

A Funny Thing Happened to Me On My Way to the Grave

The Jewish-Japanese Sex and Cook Book and How to Raise Wolves

Shut Up and Eat Your Snowshoes!

Published by POCKET BOOKS

Shut Up and Eat Your Snowshoes!

by

Jack Douglas

A KANGAROO BOOK
PUBLISHED BY POCKET BOOKS NEW YORK

SHUT UP AND EAT YOUR SNOWSHOES!

Putnam edition published 1970

POCKET BOOK edition published March, 1971

5th printing.................December, 1976

This POCKET BOOK edition includes every word contained in the original, higher-priced edition. It is printed from brand-new plates made from completely reset, clear, easy-to-read type.
POCKET BOOK editions are published by
POCKET BOOKS,
a division of Simon & Schuster, Inc.,
A GULF+WESTERN COMPANY
630 Fifth Avenue,
New York, N.Y. 10020.
Trademarks registered in the United States
and other countries.

ISBN: 0-671-81117-7.
Library of Congress Catalog Card Number: 77-97082.

Cover illustration by W. Neibast.

Printed in the U.S.A.

For Bobby and Timothy—
may they never listen to their father's advice.

Shut Up and Eat Your Snowshoes!

1

ONE hot summer day in Old New Litchridge, Connecticut, I was lying under a dead palm tree, seriously considering writing a novel about two nipples named Heloise and Abelard who were mad about each other and later, when separated by a Maidenform bra, pined away and died. I thought it would make a great movie—for Twiggy. She could play Abelard. At the same time I was conjuring up this marvelous mammiferous cinematic saga, which could only be directed by Jane Fonda's husband (I would insist on that), I was leafing through the latest edition of Previews, Incorporated's catalogue of expensive real estate.

Most of what Previews had to offer was financially out of my class or in Mougins, France, or Benalmádena, Spain, or Eagle Bend, Minnesota, or Jamaica.

I had always carried on an idle flirtation with the idea of Jamaica. I could picture myself as the overseer of a vast Colombian-coffee plantation, with hundreds of Juan Valdezes handpicking each superdooper, round, full, and just ripe Colombian-coffee bean. Then later that man in the white suit with the mustache, El Exigente, would come chugging up through the steaming jungle on the old narrow-gauge railroad. He'd stop at my plantation. Feel my beans. Taste my coffee and turn it down cold.

Needless to say, El Exigente would never make the return trip on that old narrow-gauge railroad back to town. We Jamaican plantation owners don't like it when somebody feels our beans and turns them down. We don't like it at all. El Exigente would soon become part of the Caribbean's vast fertilizer project.

1

There was a time, a couple of years ago, when I dashed down to Ocho Rios to investigate a 50- by 70-foot plot *nearby* Ocho Rios (the ad read) which was selling for the unbelievable low price of $23,000 (with beach privileges). When I got there, I found out the beach was 17 miles way. Uphill. On another island.

Even if this 50- by 70-foot paradise had been all the real estate romanticist had promised, we couldn't have emigrated there anyway, because Jamaica, like present-day Victorian England, does not admit dogs unless they are held in quarantine for six months to be certain the animals are not rabid. This idiocy persists even though it is a scientific reality that dogs are at the bottom of the top ten when it comes to carrying rabies. Cattle are the chief carriers of this inconvenient disease. Cattle and almost every other mammal, including man, are more apt to start foaming at the mouth and biting everybody within range than a dog. But cattle and every other mammal, including man, are admitted to Jamaica without question, and without too much inquiry into their states of health. There are only two requirements deemed absolutely essential for entry by the Jamaicans to their hostile little independency—cattle must be fat, and man must be loaded.

The injustice of this moldy rabies law, even though I had long ago decided against moving to this Caribbean isle, prompted a lengthy and not too one-sided correspondence with the Prime Minister of Jamaica, the Honorable Hugh Shearer, who, despite my snowing him under with tons of medical and scientific literature offering proof positive of the outmoded thinking of Jamaica and other holdouts in the Commonwealth of Nations, in regard to this almost nonexistent malady (in dogs anyway), was not convinced. I tried to point out to the Honorable Hugh Shearer that while the customs and the immigration and the health officials were so bloody busy seizing and quarantining a couple of sterile cocker spaniels, hundreds of rabid tourists slip into his tight little island unnoticed, until they suddenly spoil some Montego Bay Strawberry Festival and Steel Band concert by snapping at other tourists like hors d'oeuvres.

This could not only kill the tourist trade, but it could alter the taste trend in the hors d'oeuvres trade. People could switch from little pig sausages on a stick to midgets on a skewer. Think about that, Honorable Hugh Shearer, and beware of any limbo dancer who's foaming at the mouth while she's bending over backward on the floor and *not* brushing her teeth.

I studied the new Previews catalogue carefully. I didn't want to miss any exotic, impossible, end-of-the-world, insane hideaway. I had always wanted a place which you could not get to from here. Or anywhere. I combed the Florida sections (East Coast, Central, and Gulf Coast), California, New Jersey and Pennsylvania, Midwest and Ranch States, Mexico, the Bahamas and Bermuda, France, Italy, Ethiopia, Spain, Liberia, Saudi Arabia, and the Brownsville section of Brooklyn. Some clown wanted to unload a Black Panther headquarters "which would lend itself to a winter resort" (marvelous for après-ski pot parties), the ad read.

Finally I turned a page, and *there it was:* "Canada! Hunting and Fishing Lodge! Surrounded by four thousand square miles of Crown Land! Your own islands! Your own peninsula! Your own private road!" I couldn't wait. The very next day after two two-hour flights from New York's LaGuardia Airport, I found myself aboard a Cessna 180, a single-engine craft, flying over the most beautifully rugged country I had ever seen, dotted with what seemed like thousands of blue, green, and gray lakes.

The pilot, Charlie Burke, pointed straight ahead and yelled something above the roar of the engine.

"What?" I said. "I can't hear you." Then I indicated the Cessna's engine. Charlie promptly reached down and switched something, and the engine stopped, the propeller settling down to a lazy spin.

"Jesus Christ!" I screamed. "The engine stopped!"

"I know," said Charlie. "I switched it off—don't worry. This thing will glide for hours."

"I don't wanna glide," I sniveled. "I wanna *fly*—to Lost Lake!"

"Beautiful lake," said Charlie. "One of the prettiest around this part of Canada. Good fishin', too. You like to fish?"

"No," I said.

"Jeez," said Charlie. "Helluva long way to come not to fish. You hunt?"

"No," I said. "And it's a helluva long way to come not to hunt."

"I was about to say that," said Charlie. "Funny." Then he switched the engine back on. I was afraid to ask him what he'd said in the first place. I didn't want to miss anything, but being up in a plane with a glider nut made me think twice about my creed. It's what Emerson said. For those millions of you who don't remember Emerson or what he said he said, "If you're afraid to do something, do it." I'm afraid to fly, but I do it, but I didn't know out of the thousands of bush pilots in Canada, I would pick one who was an engine switcher-offer.

Again Charlie yelled something, and before I reacted, he switched off the engine and said, "Do you like to fly?"

"Only with Amelia Earhart," I shrieked. By the time Charlie had digested this we were gliding about four feet above the treetops and scattering hawks, eagles, and nesting ravens in all directions. The treetops had taken on a clutching look as I stared in horrid fascination. Just as we were about to tiptoe through the tulips of the northern tundra, Charlie switched the engine on again and we zoomed what seemed like straight up. It was the first time straight up felt good.

Another twenty minutes, and we were approaching Lost Lake. I wanted to ask Charlie why they called it Lost Lake, but I felt that God might be a little fed up with my fervencies, and I promised myself if I ever had to fly with Charlie again, I would get myself a prayer wheel with blades which I could hold outside the plane window and spin prayers a helluva lot faster than I could when I needed them most—which was all the time when flying with Charlie. I was to live to find out.

Lost Lake, from the air, was all that Previews claimed it was. It was deep blue surrounded by thick growths of white pine, red pine, hemlock, and cedar, punctuated in a lovely way with groupings of white birch and aspen. These trees seemed to be growing right out of solid rock and here and there the outcroppings were entirely bare and it was easy to see how the thousands of lakes of Canada's Cambrian Shield were gouged into being by the late great glacier.

According to Previews, there are thirteen islands in Lost Lake. As Charlie was landing, I had my head between my knees so I couldn't count them. The state I was in by that time I couldn't even count my knees.

After bouncing off the water a few times, Charlie decided to stop clowning around and brought the Cessna to a sloshing halt by bumping the heavy rubber pontoon guards against the forward side of a large wooden dock. I raised my head and looked out and there it was. Paradise!

The main lodge of the Lost Lake camp is on a small island connected to a pine- and birch-covered peninsula, which is also covered by a dozen or so varnished log buildings consisting mainly of cozy cabins heated and lighted and fully furnished with heavy rustic woodsy-type furniture.

I spent most of the time of my inspection tours in the main lodge staring out the tremendous picture windows. I was hypnotized by the disorganized beauty of the northern Ontario wild lands. I examined nothing in the main lodge. I didn't even care whether there was a toilet or whether it worked. I must have felt that in this pristine setting I would never have to go to the bathroom.

In less than twenty minutes I had decided. This was it. This was *home*. Our place in Connecticut had suddenly become a Holiday Inn where we had just been marking time till we could move to Lost Lake.

Things didn't quite work out that way. Even after I had used my number one son Bobby's college money to make a small down payment, Reiko was adamant. She wasn't going to leave our comfortable little cottage in Old New Litchridge to go to the ends of the earth with me. I explained that northern Ontario was not the ends of the earth, although when you were there it seemed like it, and I'll drink to that, after fifty years of civilization.

Months passed and I finally discovered Reiko's main objection to living in the big woods. It wasn't that the nearest neighbor was 60 miles away, stores 100, and Bobby's school not much closer. It took me a long time, but one night it came out at a party at Jack Paar's house. I was listening to some looped screenwriter explaining to those of us who would listen why Otto Preminger couldn't be a Nazi because he was an Arab. At the same time Reiko was telling Bob Goulet and his wife (the lovely Sarah Lawrence) that the reason she didn't want to live in the Canadian bush was the log cabins and in Japan only the poorest peasants live in log cabins. Then Bob Goulet said, "Abraham Lincoln lived in a log cabin."

"Was he poor?" said Reiko.

Bob Goulet changed the subject by singing the entire score of *Camelot*. When he had finished two hours later, Reiko said, "Was he poor?"

Bob Goulet didn't know any more complete scores, so he said, "Yes."

Things remained at a standstill until one day, Mr. Albert, the recently former owner of the Lost Lake place, sent me some lovely color photographs of the property. As soon as Reiko saw the bridge connecting the little island to the peninsula, she said, "It's beautiful—just like Japan!" I failed to get any connection because the bridge is just a plain log-supported span with a plank floor, but it *was* painted a sort of Oriental red—the same color they used to use on temple blocks when I was a drummer— so this may have been what she meant. Mr. Albert had suggested that we go up there for a weekend in January. Reiko thought this was a jolly idea. I wasn't too sure. I immediately contacted my friend Jean-Luc Bombardier in Valcourt, Quebec, who had recently returned from an expedition to the North Pole by snowmobile. I asked him if he had any suggestions for Lost Lake in January. He suggested don't go— or warm clothing.

2

ON January 20, Charlie Burke flew us into Lost Lake. He didn't shut off the engine this time. And he didn't do much pointing either. I thought he was rather tense and grim about the whole thing, so like a fool, I asked him what was the matter. This was the mistake of my life. It seems on takeoff from Lake Tyburn (the plane was now equipped with skis instead of pontoons) one of the skis had been torn loose. (They had told him over the radio.) I now seemed to be able to make myself heard very well over the noise of the engine. I screamed, "What are we gonna do when we get to Lost Lake? How are we gonna land?"

"Somehow," Charlie said.

This wasn't good enough for me. I again screamed above the engine, "Why don't we go back and land at Lake Tyburn near the base? If anything happens, they'll help us."

"No," said Charlie. "If I make a bad landing, I don't want anybody to see it. I don't want to spoil my record."

"Good God!" I yelled. "How can you make a good landing with one ski?"

Charlie looked at me a long moment, then yelled calmly, "When I give the word, everybody *lean*."

A few minutes later it started to snow. I nudged Charlie to get his attention, then pointed at the blizzard we were now in the midst of.

Charlie said, "Just *lean*."

We started spinning wildly across what I hoped was ice. Then the plane stopped, slightly tilted on its left wing.

I said to Charlie, "Now?" and he said, "Yeah." So we all leaned to the right and the plane leveled itself. Charlie smiled the quiet smile of a man who has done his job.

"Where are we?" I said.

His quiet smile faded, and he looked at me with equal parts of irritation and tolerance. "Lost Lake," he said. "The camp is that way," pointing at the swirling curtain of blizzard.

"You mean we have to walk?" said Reiko.

"I wanna use my skis," said Bobby.

"Snowshoes would be better," said Charlie.

"Great," I said. "We got six pairs of snowshoes—all at the camp."

"Well," said Charlie, practically, "we'll just hafta go get 'em," and started off through the snow in the direction of nowhere. Reiko, Bobby, and I, with no great desire to spend the winter with a one-ski airplane in the middle of a frozen lake, quickly slogged after him.

After what seemed like a week and a half of lifting our feet up and over or almost over three feet of snow, we started climbing the rock, which was our main island. My opinion of Charlie changed immediately. I now classed him with the Vikings—and a seeing-eye dog. How he ever found the island in the face of that howling storm only God knows.

"Well, just call on the radio when you wanna come back to town," said Charlie. "I gotta take off before this storm gets *bad*."

"What about that broken ski?" I yelled above the gale.

"Oh," he said, "funny how you forget." Then he turned to Reiko. "Got a hairpin?"

"What the hell—" I said.

"I need a hairpin to open the toolbox," said Charlie. Reiko gave him a hairpin and he swirled away into the unknown. And a half hour later his plane clipped the tops of our tallest red pines.

"There goes Charlie," said Reiko. Which, I felt, is about as much as anyone could have said at the time.

According to the mercury in the thermometer on the living-room wall, the temperature inside the lodge was 32 degrees—below zero. Bobby started to cry and Reiko looked grim as only wives can when the husband has entangled them once more in an inescapable web of tragic circumstance (which happens daily in most marriages).

"Well," I said, trying to sound like an Edgar Guest poem, "I guess I'd better get a fire started." I'm sure that Reiko's being Japanese was the only reason she didn't say, "Why don't you set fire to the whole place!" But the Japanese are too polite for that. Actually it would have been the *only* way to get warm.

I forced the door against the wind and pushed my way to the woodpile. We had about three cords of birchwood stacked and buried under an enormous snowdrift. After I kicked away enough snow to get to the wood, I discovered that all the logs were frozen to one another. It was as if I had ordered three cords of firewood welded into one unit. By this time I was sweating inside my heavy wolfskin parka, but my hands had become two fossilized hooks, with no noticeable function. Now I was getting desperate. What had I done? I had torn my darling little wife and my precious little son from a life of Connecticut ease and dragged them north into a cruel and pitiless land to freeze to death—just because the neighborhood kids in Old New Litchridge kept blowing up our mailbox. Here our mailbox was 116 miles away. As the vulture flies. I knew it was up to me to keep my family alive. I felt my way toward the boathouse, which contained all sorts of tools. It was a tough fight through the snow, which by this time was a double blizzard (a meteorology term I made up, but this storm could not be called anything else—the Blizzard of '88 was a flurry).

The boathouse was deep with snow from a broken window, but I managed to poke around under it and find an old tire iron and struggle back to the cordwood, much against the will of my lungs. Too many years of nonhabit-forming cigarettes were cutting my breath to short painful gasps, interspersed with flashes of total black. I thought: *Maybe this is it.* The effort was so great.

In no less than a half hour I had pried five or six logs from their fellows and from one another. They were heavy with ice, so I brought them to the lodge door one at a time. The last trip was marked by several abrupt bone-crunching falls, and when I reached the door, as I was about to pound with my tire iron, it opened suddenly and I found myself sprawled on the living-room floor. It was a scene from Sergeant Preston of the Yukon when I opened my eyes almost immediately and said, "Where am I?"

Reiko said, "Take off your coat, dinner's ready."

I couldn't believe it. There was a roaring fire in the fireplace, and the table was set with steaming plates of Irish stew, looking like breast of pheasant in the soft glow of candlelight.

"Where'd you get the wood?" I said.

"In the woodbox."

"What woodbox?"

"That woodbox," said Bobby. "Right next to the fireplace."

"Jesus H. Christ," I said.

"That's what Mommy said," said Bobby. "Papa—what does the *H* stand for?"

"Hashimoto," I said.

"That's what Mommy said. That used to be her name before she married you."

"Shut up, Bobby," Reiko said, "and eat your Irish stew—it'll put hair on your chest."

"I hope so," Bobby said. "It'll keep me warm on the way to school."

After we had eaten, we felt better. The cabin was getting warmer and outside the snow had stopped and a lovely full moon lighted the beautiful silent white world with shimmering silveriness. The North Star was almost directly overhead. A wolf howled. What a beautiful lonely sound! From that moment Connecticut ceased to exist. If it ever had.

3

OUR test weekend at Lost Lake was not a smashing success. Although the cold abated somewhat (the mercury crept up to about 15 below and stayed there), the sun remained hidden and the whole world so far as we knew was a sullen leaden gray. The shores of the lake were edged in a black border of pine, cedar, and spruce. There was no color anywhere except in the tips of our cherry noses. Our indoor toilet was frozen solid and the ice had neatly halved the bowl, because our caretaker, one Jake Moon, whom we inherited from the previous owner, had simply neglected to drain the water out of it before the big freeze.

Jake was supposed to have met us when we arrived at Lost Lake, but so far we had not seen him. At first we hoped that nothing had happened to him; then after we had examined our toilet-circle, we hoped it had. More—much more—about this un-Admirable Crichton later.

Reiko was a fair sport about the cold, the stove, and the outdoor plumbing, but she said it was too lonely.

"Not enough people," she said.

"I don't understand," I said. "In Connecticut you used to complain about too many people."

"I don't mean that—I like to go to the store every day and buy the groceries."

This was something I never knew. It had always seemed to me that Reiko had gone to the store too much in Connecticut, and when I asked her why she didn't buy a whole week's supplies in one day, the answer was always scrambled. Now I knew what it was—in Japan, with the lack of refrigeration, everyone shopped every day. This was a habit that she was born with. It was a very congenital thing. It was a Japanese compulsion comparable to the American housewife who cannot drive a station wagon without a cigarette dangling from her lips. Another very congenital thing.

"Reiko," I said, "you knew when we came up here that you couldn't go to the store every day—it's more than a hundred miles away!"

"Before we came up here, you said it was only ninety."

"I *lied*—I wanted you to like this place."

"I like this place," said Bobby, who had just come in and shaken off at least his own weight in snow on the living-room floor. "I saw a moose!"

"Where?" said Reiko, struggling into her coat and boots.

"You wanna see the moose, Mommy?" said Bobby.

"Where is it?"

"It's right in back of Papa's office."

He was referring to the cabin I decided to use as an office just in case I ever could leave off hauling firewood long enough to write a few words.

We all dashed outside and moved stealthily toward my "office."

"There's the moose," said Bobby.

"I don't see him," said Reiko.

"Neither do I," I said.

"Right there!" said Bobby, irritably. "Next to that tree!"

"What tree?" I said. "There's at least twenty million trees in the direction you're pointing."

"What a lousy Mama and Papa!" Bobby said.

"Bobby," I said, "you're not supposed to call your lousy Mama and Papa *lousy!*"

"Not even if you can't see the moose?"

"No."

Just then we heard a sound like an ocean liner followed by a series of snorts, and sure enough, a moose, at least the size of an oil tanker, walked into an open space between the trees. Almost at the same time he got wind of us and turned and disappeared into the bush.

"He was beautiful," said Reiko in a very impressed tone.

"That's what I keep telling you," I said. "Who needs people?"

Before Reiko could challenge this, Bobby said, "I wanna moose."

I said, "You've already got a Malemute, a Pomeranian, five wolves, and a cougar. What the hell would you do with a moose? Who'd take care of it?"

"*I* would," Bobby said. "I'd feed it every day and I'd take it for walks."

"Okay," I said. "We'll see."

"*We'll see!*" Bobby snorted. "That's what you said when I wanted a *tyrannosaurus!*"

4

THE most necessary of evils—and the most evil of necessaries —is a moving-van company. Especially if you expect to get tons of nonessential accumulation from one mortgage *avec maison* to another. All of you who are reading this have had an experience with a moving-van company, so I shall spare you no detail. Your first contact with the Dalton Gang, doing business under the pseudonym "The Plymouth Rock Moving Company" will be something called the "Estimator" who is a little old man with half-inch-thick glasses who "estimates" that you have about 10,000 pounds of household goods. "We always *over*estimate," Mr. Fullger, our friendly neighborhood estimator, told us. "So I don't think it will run anywhere near that." Then he chuckled, confidently. We found out later why he chuckled and why he was confident.

After the estimator leaves, hundreds of cardboard boxes, cartons, barrels, and wardrobes arrive. When I asked Mr. Fullger if we would get anything back on these articles after we had finished with them, Mr. Fullger said, "Yes, if you can get them back from Canada to us here in Old New Litchridge." Then he chuckled confidently. This made twice.

Reiko, Bobby, and I did the packing, which delivered us from having to squander our life savings on this frivolity. If we had paid *them* to do the packing, we wouldn't have been able to move.

By the time we had finished packing, Reiko and Bobby and I were not speaking to one another, and Tanuki and four other younger wolves, which we had recently acquired, Pussycat, the cougar, Chibi, the Malemute, and Doggie, the Pomeranian, cringed in fear for their lives at feeding time—because our eyes were wilder than theirs. By far.

We were all now psychopathic ogres, but we had the satisfaction of knowing that we had done our part in behalf of our life savings. They were still intact. But not for long.

Early in the morning of a bright spring day when the moving van was supposed to arrive in Chinookville, we were sitting on the dock of Canada Goose Airways, eagerly awaiting our first glimpse of the big yellow Plymouth Rock van with the big green letters WE TREAT YOUR GOODS LIKE GOODIES painted on its sides. We waited from early in the morning of that bright spring day until late in the evening of a gloomy, drizzly, chilly, depressing spring night. Our goodies did not arrive. Mr. McArdle of Canada Goose Airways sadly informed us that the big PBY plane we had standing by to transport our stuff from Chinookville to Lost Lake would have to leave. It had been chartered for the next day to fly a group of Eskimos to New York to appear on *What's My Line?*

I told Mr. McArdle that I understood. I also understood that to have the PBY standing by for a full day had cost us $500. I further understood by all the omens that our life savings would have been safer in a shoe box at the Alamo.

One week later a plane landed at Lost Lake, and Charlie Burke taxied her up to our airplane dock, neatly sideswiping a canoe in which I happened to be playing Hiawatha. Reiko and Bobby and Chibi and Doggie rushed down to the dock, while Jake stood by, not too ready to load some empty oil and gasoline drums for the return trip to Chinookville. Charlie's first words were: "Holy cow! I never saw so many boxes and cartons and stuff in my life! You folks musta had a mighty big place back there in the States."

"It wasn't so big, Charlie," I said. "It just seemed big the first of every month."

"That's pretty funny," Charlie said. "But I've heard funnier."

"Is the furniture here?" Reiko said, her beautiful brown eyes sparkling with anticipation.

"It sure is, Mrs. Douglas," Charlie said. "We're stacking it at the hangar. Ever since that PBY left, we're stuck. We gotta bring it in by smaller planes. Hafta make a lot of trips."

I must have groaned.

"Whatsamatter, Jack?" Charlie said. "Smaller planes are cheaper. Only fifty cents a mile."

"Yeah," I said. "And with those small planes, we oughta be all moved in by next Easter."

"Relax," Charlie said. "You're not in New York now—time doesn't mean a damn thing up here."

"I wish you'da said 'mileage' or 'money' instead of 'time,' " I said. "Then maybe I could relax."

"That's better, Jack, you're gettin' funnier," Charlie said. "Now—you wanna fly up and see the big mess . . . and pay the moving-van man?"

"Yeah," I said. "Maybe we'll crash on the way."

"You'll never crash with me," Charlie said. "I've been flyin' over this bush for twenty-five years."

"Wait'll they find out you haven't got a license," I said.

"That's the funniest yet, Jack."

The flight from Lost Lake to Chinookville Lake was, as Willie Sutton used to say after a successful bank job, uneventful outside of Charlie's playing "Chicken" with a long wedge of migrating geese who were flying in the *opposite* direction. The geese didn't veer off course one inch, which I can understand—because they had been flying this route a lot longer than Charlie and his Cessna. Charlie's heart-stopping dive at the last possible moment was the only thing that saved us from landing in a treetop and up to our untidy buttocks in genuine Canadian goose liver.

The bill from the movers shocked me, as I guess I knew it would. Our friendly neighborhood estimator had been off about 5,000 pounds. I hope when he dies, someone will have the good taste to engrave WE ALWAYS OVERESTIMATE on his tombstone. Then maybe they can have a little tape machine like they do at Forest Lawn, playing his confident chuckle eternally.

Actually, the overestimation ploy did not ruffle me half so much as the "extra" charges—all itemized in Sanskrit. A few items I managed, from my days as an Egyptologist, to decode. There were tidy little expensive and untraceable tidbits such as: "Additional Transportation Charge $74.75." This was rather esoteric, I thought. What did it mean? Did the driver make a side trip to Niagara Falls for a couple of days so our love seat could have a honeymoon? This item was given an air of legitimacy by the cryptic annotation "Rule 170." Rule 170 exists only, I'm sure, in the inaccessible (to the skewered consignee) dreambook of the moving company and is kept in a velvet safe in a faerie castle in downtown Glocca Morra, which can only be opened with a golden key by a zombie elf.

Then on top of the above-mentioned "Additional Transportation Charge" there was another *additional* additional charge of $112.13 for shipments to or from Canada or Mexico, which, if we had been moving from Connecticut to New Jersey or Staten Island, would have read: "Additional Charge for Shipments to or from New Jersey or Staten Island."

I was now flat on my back on the canvas, willing to take an eight count and then get up and try again, but I changed my mind when a little item of $328.55 caught my eye. This was for "Other Service"! So far, the *other* services were beginning to add up to more than the actual transportation of our worldly goods.

I got nowhere with Ollie Gersdorf, the driver of the moving van. "I don't know what all them items are, Mr. Douglas," he said. "It's all regulated by the government."

"Yeah," I said. "So was the Spanish-American War."

"I wouldn't know about that," Ollie said. "I'm a Canadian."

"Let's hear you sing 'O Canada,' " I said.

"What's that?" he said.

"I thought you said you were a Canadian."

"I'm from Quebec," he said.

"What do you sing there?"

" 'Frère Jacques' and 'Alouette' mostly."

I'd had enough of this, so I asked him where he had been on the day he was supposed to deliver our stuff.

"Resting," he said.

"For crissakes!" I said. "*Resting*—for a whole week!"

"Well, not the whole time. I did manage to get in some golf."

"Your *resting* cost us five hundred dollars," I said.

"Sorry," Ollie said. "If only there was *something* I could do."

"How about unloading the truck?" I said.

"Oh, I couldn't do *that*," he said. "I'm just a driver. That's all. Just a driver. All I have to do is drive. The loading and unloading—that's up to somebody else."

"Like who?" I said. "The June Taylor Dancers?"

"I wouldn't know about that," he said. "I'm a Canadian."

This was apparently another well-planned nonservice of the Plymouth Rock Moving Company. This huge van had arrived at its prearranged destination, loaded with 15,000 pounds of furniture, books, kitchenware, filing cabinets, sleds, bikes, etc. ad infinitum, with no prearranged method for unloading these *now* almost priceless articles.

"I guess Reiko, Bobby, and I will have to do it then. After all, it's only fifteen thousand pounds," I said. "Couldn't possibly take more than a month at the most."

"If I leave the truck here," Ollie said, "it'll cost you a hundred dollars a day—rule number one hundred and fifty-six."

"Do you have a rule about unpremeditated homicide?" I said.

"It's all regulated by the government," he said. "Like the Spanish-American War."

"Horse manure!" I said.

"That's regulated by the government, too," Charlie said.

The stalwarts who worked as mechanics and maintenance men at Canada Goose Airways came to our rescue and unloaded the whole 15,000 pounds in less than an hour. They wouldn't take any money for this compassionate act, so I promised them a good drunk, and although I had cut down on the lovely stuff some twelve years ago, I may join them. Or better still, lead them.

Transporting our things from the hangar in Chinookville to Lost Lake became a matter of stick-to-it-iveness on the part of Canada Goose Airways. They used their three small planes to do it. Our airplane dock at Lost Lake began to have the feel of an international stopover point. Sometimes we'd have all three aircraft there at one time—one unloading and the other two a quarter mile or so offshore, waiting their turn. Charlie Burke and two other Canada Goose pilots, Big John and Jim Babb, loaded, then unloaded our things from the planes' small interiors. On some flights all they could carry would be one section of a three-sectional couch. Some items, such as my long office tables, were strapped just above the pontoons, causing the plane to fly sideways. They almost had to make a bank shot to land correctly on the lake. Charlie, Big John, and Jim Babb were geniuses. No matter what terrifying acrobatic shenanigans their clumsy loads threw them into, somehow they fluttered down from the sky onto the surface of Lost Lake like drunken autumn leaves.

With each splashdown the loons sounded off with weird stridulations of outrage and protest. I felt like doing the same thing when I thought of the astronomical bill we were running up with Canada Goose Airways. We were rapidly approaching bankruptcy at an always accelerating fifty cents per mile.

5

ONE week after helpful Ollie had magnanimously accepted my check, which put the Plymouth Rock Moving Company forever in the black, all our proud possessions were in permanent residence at Lost Lake, Ontario, Canada, where I would spend the rest of my life writing books, television specials, documentaries, sex articles, nonsex articles, cake recipes, and fortune cookies, the proceeds from all of this to be forwarded to Canada Goose Airways on account.

Summer had come to northern Ontario and it was lovely. With the nice weather, our faithful old caretaker, Jake Moon, had returned to help us, when his back, or his ulcers, or his sinuses, or his liver, or his arthritis or his monumental hangovers permitted.

Jake Moon was a wiry-looking little man, not more than five feet six in his seemingly rapidly deteriorating stockinged feet. He was about forty years old and wore glasses which had been discarded by Benjamin Franklin's grandfather. The glasses were square and at least a quarter of an inch thick, which made his eyes look as if they belonged to something swimming by a viewing window at Marineland.

"Had a real tough winter," Jake said, after his first hello.

"Oh," I said. "Where were you?"

"Here."

"Where?"

"Here—at this camp."

"All winter?" I said.

"Yeah," he said, "except when I caught the flu."

"Who'd you catch the flu from?" I said.

"Just caught it," he said.

"Jake," I said, with a feeling that this drag-ass drone would not be long in our employ, "the flu is communicable —you have to get it *from* somebody."

"Oh?" he said.

"Yeah. Anybody visit you back here—one hundred and sixteen miles back in the bush—did somebody with the flu drop in on you?"

"Yeah," he said, seizing this gift opportunity, "Mr. and Mrs. Trilby were here—they both had the flu. I *had* to catch it."

"The Trilbys live about sixty or seventy miles from here, and they're both over eighty years old. How'd they get here? The snow was over five feet deep."

"Didn't have much snow this past winter," said Jake.

"Reiko and Bobby and I were here in January and there was a good five feet of snow on the ground," I said.

"January what?" he said.

"January twentieth," I said.

"Oh, yeah," he said, "I remember. It really snowed that day. The Trilbys didn't come on that day. They're over eighty years old. They *never* would have made it. Not with the flu."

Mr. and Mrs. Trilby, of course, had never been near Lost Lake. They had lived almost all their lives in a tiny cabin on the edge of a very remote lake. They *never* came out of the bush—except during forest fires—according to Charlie Burke, so Jake Moon's fabrication was hanging out beautifully. This was our first warning that we had a sinking rat aboard the Good Ship Lollipop. Other indications of this varlet's inattention to our needs became apparent as the warm, somnolent wiles of the Canadian summer led us down the garden path to the icy arms of the northern winter. I knew that if we were to survive, this gold-bricking bastard better not be around to *help* us. But being a master procrastinator, I did nothing about it, and also we had no one else. He was the only game in town.

One of the tasks I had lined up for this inconstant Moon was the cutting of a bush road through the forest to the west of Lost Lake and connecting up to a lumber road, which would take us out to another lumber road, which would lead into a secondary road, which, if it weren't flooded or under 10 feet of snow, would lead us to the Trans-Canada Highway, which went all the way out to Vancouver, which may not sound too thrilling to those of you who have a thing for Acapulco. But to us, we would do *anything* to get to that secondary road! And when I say "anything," it included keeping Jake Moon around to slash an exit out of our locked-in pristineness.

Besides, not having done anything all winter long or even visited the camp (when he was supposed to be living there, caretaking), this bandit had talked me into raising his status from a simple dishonest caretaker, who was getting $225 per month, to the exalted position of an eight-hour-a-day workman at the unheard-of (to anyone in his right mind in this part of the country) salary of $90 a week. My mother always told me I wasn't very bright and I've spent most of my life doing nothing to louse up her opinion.

I was silly enough to suppose that this crooked wood sprite would actually put in an eight-hour day. He was *awake* for eight hours a day—I'll say that for him—but anything in the way of labor seemed the farthest thing from his Machiavellian mind. He would ooze into our living room promptly at 8 A.M., seemingly through the wall, because he never knocked, but suddenly he was there in our easiest chair, breathing his last.

"What's the matter, Jake?" I would ask.

"Nothing."

"I thought you were in pain."

"Oh, it's nothing," he would say, "just a little gallbladder attack. It should be okay by noon."

"Maybe we'd better fly you into the doctor's," I said then, as he gave off with another death rattle. "Or maybe we should go directly to the hospital."

"No," he said. "I'll be all right. I'll take a hot-water bottle with me."

"Take a hot-water bottle with you?" Reiko said. "Where?"

"Out into the woods where I gotta cut the new road with the chain saw. It weighs twenty-three pounds," he said.

Right away Reiko was all warm sympathy, or she didn't understand the situation. "Maybe the Trilbys could help you." Jake just looked at her and so did I.

"I'll fix the hot-water bottle," I said.

About ten thirty or eleven Jake would creep down to the boat dock and force himself into our fastest boat and then zoom off toward the spot he was going to cut. This spot always seemed to be behind one of the thirteen islands, so we never could see whether he actually did land on the mainland, although we would hear the whine of the chain saw clearly at, it seemed to me, carefully spaced intervals. Promptly at eleven thirty, the sound of the saw would end abruptly, and Jake would be zooming back to his quarters. Lunch.

At exactly one thirty, we could hear the rasping whir of the 25-horsepower motor as Jake hastened back to his post to put in a good two hours and fifteen minutes of honest toil, before he zoomed back to his quarters for an early dinner and an evening of Transylvanian folk songs, directly from Bela Lugosi, on his shortwave radio.

This routine went on day after day until my natural curiosity, $90-per-week's worth, began getting out of hand. I wanted to see what he was doing with that chain saw all by himself in the bush. He kept telling us that the road would be finished in a couple of weeks.

"Almost across the swamp," he announced one morning.

"What swamp?" I said.

"What swamp!" he said. "The *big* swamp!"

"What are you cutting with the chain saw in a swamp," I said, "peat?"

I think he was getting fed up with my noninterference, but he controlled himself admirably and said, "The swamp is full of trees."

"Oh," said Reiko. "Like in Louisiana."

This was all I needed. "When the hell were you in Louisiana?" I said.

"Never," she said. "I saw a picture in the *National Geographic*." It really didn't sound like *National Geographic,* but I've been interpreting this Japanese angel for a long time, so I knew what she meant.

"Those are cypress trees in Louisiana. They don't have them in Canada," I said, hoping I was right.

Jake, who never lost a chance to be helpful, said nothing. Finally, after what seemed like years of invisible chain sawing, I decided to *spy* on the road builder. I took another boat and zoomed up the lake myself until I saw the other boat; then I slyly cut off the motor and drifted to the shore, then pussyfooted into the bush. In five minutes I was sorry I had used this approach, because that's all it took for me to be hopelessly lost. If you've never experienced this, you don't know what panic is. My beloved wilderness suddenly became a silent, ominous, threatening enemy. I tried to remember Mr. Albert's mimeographed list of rules, which was tacked on the wall of every cabin. These rules were the ten commandments of survival in the bush. YOU MUST NOT COVET THY NEIGHBOR'S WIFE? That didn't sound right. DO NOT PANIC. That was more like it. Still, that *could* be part of not coveting your neighbor's wife. I was starting to remember. It was the panic that moved my brain off dead center. THERE IS NOTHING IN THE BUSH WHICH CAN HURT YOU. Scant consolation, remembering the size of the many black bears we had seen, plus a wolf which was not in the family. STAY WHERE YOU ARE AND SOMEONE FROM THE CAMP WILL FIND YOU. Who? Reiko? Bobby? Chibi? Tanuki? Doggie? Pussycat? Oh, dear God, no!—Jake????? I have to depend on *him* finding me after all I've done to him! Making him work four hours a day, five days a week! I started the Lord's Prayer and wished that I had been born a Catholic. They have a helluva lot more prayers for situations like this. IF POSSIBLE,

STAY IN A CLEARING OR AN OPEN RIDGE WHERE YOU CAN BE
SEEN BY A PLANE. That was another one of Mr. Albert's
rules. What plane? The Sault Ste. Marie-North Bay plane
which flew over at 9:30 P.M.? How could they see me? And
if they did, how would they know I was lost? And would
they stop?

After a while, frenzy had taken the place of panic. Frenzy
with a slight dash of terror and hysteria. I remembered another one of Mr. Albert's rules—*how* I don't know: BUILD A
FIRE, AND IF NIGHT IS APPROACHING, ASSEMBLE ENOUGH DRY
WOOD TO LAST UNTIL MORNING. That was all very well, but
what would I assemble so *I* would last until morning? Having
a body composed of nothing but a few unlubricated bones
lashed together with raw nerve ends, I knew I wouldn't make
it. Then I remembered something that wasn't in Mr. Albert's
sheet of rules: IF YOU ARE LOST IN THE WOODS, FIRE THREE
SHOTS. That's what I'd do. I'd wait until nine thirty and fire
three shots at the Sault Ste. Marie-North Bay plane. That
ought to stir up something. I might be arrested for shooting
down a scheduled airliner, but at least I'd be found. There
was just one thing wrong with this plan. What would I fire
the three shots *with?* I had my hunting knife. Maybe if I
stabbed three times? No. That just wouldn't be the same.
I was finished. I sat down on a glaciated rock and waited
for the grim reaper. In twenty minutes he showed up. With a
chain saw.

"I thought I heard something," Jake said. The sonofabitch
had ears like radar. The only thing they didn't do was spin
around. They just twitched.

"Yeah," I said. "I thought I'd come over and watch you
saw down a tree."

"Yeah," he said. "Good idea, but it's quitting time. I'm
knocking off early today. It's Friday. The end of the week.
I'm going into town. Going to a funeral."

"Gee," I said, "I'm sorry." Then I suddenly thought: *If he's
been out here in the bush for the past five days, how would
he know about a funeral?*

"Whose funeral you going to?"

"Have to wait till I get to town," he said.

I'll never learn. I always ask.

The reason Jake wanted to knock off early, we found out,
was that he wanted to get dressed in his Sunday best, which

took him quite awhile. When he finally made it, Reiko, Bobby, Chibi, Doggie, and I went down to the dock to sing "Aloha" as he zoomed off toward the other end of the lake and freedom.

As we turned toward the lodge with a happy feeling of relief at having the place all to ourselves for two whole days, we suddenly heard a sound like a crunching shot, and we looked out on the lake, and there was Jake in the boat going end over end, with a tremendous splash, for a finish.

He'd run into a huge turtle.

It took two hours of mouth-to-mouth resuscitation, but the turtle finally started to breathe normally again.

6

THE toughest thing about living back in the woods is explaining to your friends *why*. Every time we see people from the outside they are astounded that: (1) we are still alive; (2) we are still healthy; and (3) we look happy. This not only astounds them—it annoys them. What kind of nut would take a beautiful young wife and a six-year-old child to live in the outback of the Canadian wilderness? Me.

"Isn't it lonely?" they say, daring you to say No when the answer is Yes.

"Life is passing you by—*way* up there!" The only reply to this is "Amen."

"Don't you miss seeing people? Doesn't *human contact* mean anything to you?" If this means would I like to reach out and give Raquel Welch a pat on the ass, the answer is Yes.

And I'm sure Reiko misses the challenge and excitement of living dangerously in the parking lot at the A & P, but neither of us misses the human contact we experienced last winter with a driveway snow-plower-outer in Old New Litchridge, after a particularly heavy snowfall, which turned me into an instant misanthrope.

Because I had the audacity to suggest to this jeep jackal, when he had finished and I had paid him the $25 ransom, that I *still* could not possibly drive my car out of the driveway, because the snow removal had been insufficient, he mumbled something that sounded exactly like "fussy prick," under his breath, and zoomed away into the night and to the next $25 boob.

While we were sleeping, he returned and pushed all the snow back into the driveway.

I was so incensed by this new turn of suburban treachery I called a cheap triggerman to take care of this Judas. The triggerman, who had retired on a pension from Murder, Incorporated, said the fee would be $12, but when I told him who the target was, he reduced this to $9 or two for $18, which was the wholesale rate for Old New Litchridge. Or if I could get twenty-three more boobs besides myself, he would give me the charter rate. This was easily arranged.

Another human contact which doesn't mean too much to me or *any*one stuck back in Old New Litchridge is the whelp at Gristede's, who, after this same strenuous snowstorm, told a widow with three sick children, "We only *deliver* to our regular customers!" and slammed the phone down. The charm and mien of this fair-weather fink is no doubt one of the reasons the merchants of Old New Litchridge had to get together and offer a chance of a free trip to Bermuda to anyone who shopped in Old New Litchridge and got the lucky number.

This little scheme backfired somewhat—the woman who shopped in Old New Litchridge and got the lucky number and the free trip to Bermuda now does *all* her shopping *there*. It's cheaper. And a helluva lot politer.

By living in an uncharted area of the world, and sidestepping the use, as much as possible, of modern-day transportation, I avoid the machinations of the automotive world and their local emissaries, the car dealers, who sweet-talk you into dipping into capital you haven't received yet to buy a brand shiny new car with a five-year or 50,000-mile warranty, which means that *if* at *any time* within five years, or 50,000 miles (whichever comes first), your brand shiny new car suddenly reverts and turns back into a *pumpkin,* you are *fully covered.* They give you another pumpkin. Which is safe at any speed.

Another human contact I do not miss is our friendly neighborhood junkie, who broke into our former castle regularly to pick up our television set for delivery to our friendly neighborhood fence, where he would exchange it for enough money to give to our friendly neighborhood pusher for a friendly neighborhood fix. Incidentally, this unforgettable character stopped visiting *us* after we let the cougar act as watchdog one night, while we were out. We came home to find Pussycat playing mouse with an unfamiliar and very ragged nose.

When things don't go quite the way I imagined they should up here in the bush, I wonder if the whole thing is a mistake. When this happens, I bring my mind back into line by remembering the day back in Old New Litchridge when the "insurance investigator" crossed the demilitarized zone into our territory. I had just pulled into the driveway, after an hour of breaststroking at the YMCA (it's a new course for the fellows who don't like the water), when an unkempt individual wearing an all-weather mod ensemble and tennis shoes walked from our front door toward a ripple-fendered, rust-trimmed 1957 Chevy, with what looked like a human scalp dangling from its radio antenna. Before this interloper could start his car, I drove in right in back of it and blocked any chance of an exit. Then I got out and asked, in my best Inspector Erskine of the FBI voice, "May I help you?" And flashed my Green Stamp book at him.

This bothered him not one bit. "I'm an insurance investigator," he said.

"Fine," I said, "come back next week—after the fire." The hooligan in his permanent-wrinkle suit apparently didn't think this was sidesplitting, so I said, "Give me your identification," as versus *"Show* me your identification." An oral distinction I had learned in my youth while working as a doorman for a Bakersfield, California, drive-in massage parlor. The "insurance investigator" opened up an imitation cardboard wallet and waved a crumpled something at me. I said, *"Give* me your identification!" I was working myself up nicely, because this tatterdemalion had had the insufferable gall to ignore my no trespassing sign, which was a little hard to do, because it read: TRESPASSERS WILL BE CRUCIFIED! UPSIDE DOWN! Printed in both English and Latin.

"Didn't you see the sign?" I said, my voice cracking a bit because I wasn't entirely into the role.

"I see lotsa signs," he said. "I'm an insurance investigator," handing me his leprous wallet. After I had it in my hands, I wished I had not been so hasty. With Father Damien gone who could I turn to? I had visions of spending the rest of the day in a hot sheep-dip bubble bath, but I carried bravely on and examined his identification. It consisted solely of a card he had bought at the five-and-dime in the last century and had the words "Insurance Investigator" printed on it in disappearing ink. That's all the ragged piece of cardboard said. If he was representing a certain insurance company, this was a well-guarded secret, because this information was missing. Also, the signature line was bare, as was the little square space meant to be occupied by an identifying photo.

"Where's your picture?" I said.

"Oh," he said, "I can explain that." But he didn't, so I called the cops. They were even more suspicious than I was, especially after Reiko relayed the information that this man had tried to force his way into the house to "inspect" it.

The Old New Litchridge police checked him out thoroughly and found that he *was* an insurance investigator and also a general all-around snoop for other groups. We never found out what he was investigating, but the Maryland Casualty Insurance Company canceled my house insurance the very next day. This was extremely frustrating, because even a sweetheart of a guy like the old triggerman couldn't be expected to wipe out an entire insurance company. They might cancel *his* policy.

These few minor happenings, which I've been able to recall, don't seem like much of an excuse or a reason to forget the whole "civilized" scene, but it isn't the roar of Niagara which has changed the course of the lives of men—it's the bleep-bloop of the dripping faucet.

What else are we avoiding by burying ourselves 116 miles back in the Canadian wilds? Boredom. I wish I were there to hear the loud ho-ho-ho's of anyone who reads this. Maybe *you* aren't bored. Maybe *you* get a thrill a minute sitting in a Stygian discothèque watching underdeveloped or overdeveloped female buttocks trying unsuccessfully to simulate the mating movements of a virgin baboon. Not that I've ever *seen* a virgin baboon mating, because I haven't been to the movies lately, but I'm sure it would be a lot more sensual than anything the *now* generation has been able to sweat up.

I must say that being so isolated, I miss the many opportunities I used to have to advise and counsel and guide the young people I knew. There was no generation gap so far as *we* were concerned. I do feel a great responsibility toward them, and sometimes it distresses me to think that *some* of them will forget all I've taught them. They will revert back to being unbathed, unshaved, guitar-playing boys and girls, with never a care for the future, and before they know it, they'll be unbathed, unshaved, guitar-playing old men and old ladies—too weak to picket and too arthritic to strum, with an insufficient supply of Airwick to sustain life. And Joan Baez will have a kid who grows up and goes to work for the Internal Revenue Service, whose first assignment is to arrest his mother. Her other kid will be a captain in the ROTC.

Where will the *Now* generation be *Then?*

If I may, I would like to reverse the trend of this chapter and put forth another viewpoint, and maybe people will stop asking, "What are you running away *from?*" and say, "What are you running *to?*" This list could be endless, but to narrow it down to a few basics—beyond the obvious benefits of atmosphere with a little oxygen in it, I ran away to a lovely, soul-healing *solitude.* Very few of us realize that we need solitude. We have been so brainwashed, so as to accept without question the man-is-not-an-island theory, that very few of us can escape the gravity pull of this canard. What happens to anyone who has *made* it? He wastes no time at all in isolating himself from almost everyone. Howard Hughes is not the exception. He is merely the most publicized solitudinarian. There are hundreds and maybe thousands of people like him.

Banding together in sweaty groups has become a stupid habit. A holdover from the days when people had to crowd into walled cities for their own protection. They are still jammed into walled cities, but they've been learning, especially in the last few years, that the only protection they need is from one another. A stagecoach ride through hostile Indian country was like a picnic with Mary Poppins compared to a subway journey in Fun City. All the savage redman would do, if he caught you, would be to strip you naked, then spread-eagle you out in the hot desert sun and drive a sharp stake through your belly. This is not a pleasant experience, but at least you would get some attention. If only from buzzards.

Ever seen anyone stripped naked, spread-eagled, with a stake driven through his belly in a New York subway? No one pays the slightest heed to this sort of divertissement, and they're usually pretty annoyed if they have to step over you to get to the door when it comes to their stop.

Man does not need man—not continuously at any rate. Of course, if you are not in some way financially independent, this policy of happy hermitism will be shot to hell. This still does not mean overfraternization, unless you are in the un-fortunate position of being a shoe salesman, or an insurance peddler, or a nursery school kid pushing airplane glue. Then, of course, you *have* to mix.

Anthropologists, who find out everything before everybody else and then don't tell us, have long known that human beings are not *neighborly* at all! Of course, this is borne out by the fact that some of those ancient caves (the ones with the crazy Picasso pictographs) were too tiny for other than a man and his wife (or whatever they were known as in those days) and maybe a couple of small children.

An anthropologist, who lived in Old New Litchridge and with whom I had a speaking acquaintance, during our noon-day swims at the Y was an acute observer of the human race, such as it was in Old New Litchridge. He didn't miss a thing. Personally, I have a feeling that he was less of an anthropologist and more of a voyeur, which was easy to do in a town just loaded with exhibitionists. This is probably unjust. Maybe they *do* forget to draw the drapes before they disrobe in front of their huge picture windows accompanied by a stereo record-ing of "The Battle Hymn of the Republic," played on bongo drums. Be all this free entertainment as it may, I had a great deal of respect for Dr. Robbins' opinion—I think mainly because he had a very bulgy forehead, and my grandmother always told me that *that* meant brains (I found out later that when Dr. Robbins was a child he had been flung through the windshield of a Volkswagen by a mother whose specialty was not defensive driving). Dr. Robbins informed me—and the rest of the wrecks in the Y locker room—that man is a loner and only joins others of his species because he wants something from them. If he wanted nothing, he could live his entire life without the slightest desire to join a committee. Or a bowling team. This is the way I feel. This does not mean I am antisocial (I wish, reviewing my life, that I *had* been, in a number of instances), but it does mean that I *must* choose my time and my companions. I will not, under any circumstances, anymore, go to a cozy little cocktail party for 150 people in a one-bedroom apartment, or a dinner party scheduled for eight, to which you sit down to eat at ten thirty (surrounded by brilliant drunks). If I am going to eat, it will be at my home, with friends and enemies or both, but they will be mentally stimulating and not too drunk—*before* dinner. After dinner they can get stoned. I'll be outside looking at the stars or the northern lights or the rain or the snow; then I'll sauna myself for twenty minutes and go to bed and sleep the way I used to when I had a father and a mother.

I will *not* go to New York anymore. My last visit to the city where I enjoyably misspent my youth turned me off forever.

I had had the misfortune to be trapped in Welfare Heaven by circumstances beyond my control. I had been asked by Hugh Downs to appear on *Today* to show some movies of my wolves. The *Today* show is one of the oddities of the television show—it is *live*, and it starts at 7 A.M.

Being a careful man, I knew I could not depend on my new 50,000-mile or five-year-guaranteed (whichever comes first) pumpkin to get me to the studio from our Old New Litchridge home on time, so I played it safe and stayed in New York at the St. Regal Hotel. (This is not the actual name of the hotel, but to save them the embarrassment of losing a libel suit, I have changed it somewhat.)

The desk clerk at the St. Regal, a faggot Nero, was patient with me for all of fifteen seconds as I stammered out my name and my request for the reservation I had made some three months before. By the time I made myself semiclear to his eminence he had washed his hands of me and was drying them on his toga. But in the heat of a sweltering summer's day, and with the knowledge that I was dying of a malignant sweat, I was persistent, and finally after much self-debate and doubt, this Caesarian queen allowed me to register for the Cecil Beaton Suite, which was all they had left.

"What about Cecil?" I asked.

"Not at this price," he sneer-smirked.

The Cecil Beaton Suite was lovely and was filled with his marvelous photos of the royal family. The bedroom was not to be believed. It was the only time in my life I ever slept in a swan.

New York, a joy to visit if you need a delicate brain operation or some other excuse, is always the same. The buses and shop-windows all feature a photograph of a beautifully chic female dressed in the latest fashion and the caption proclaims: "The New York woman." Then you go out into the street expecting to glimpse this gorgeous creature on every boulevard, in every exciting restaurant, in every smart Madison or Fifth Avenue shop, but whom do you see on every boulevard, in every exciting restaurant and every smart Madison and Fifth Avenue shop? A slob in a mini-dress—revealing two knockwurst legs ending in orthopedic shoes, wearing a $1,000 mink stole, a $750 blond real palomino-hair wig, under a Cossack hat, which wouldn't look good on a Cossack. Her hands feature an eighty-four-carat diamond ring she bought right after her husband dropped dead at his buttonhole machine, and her fingernails are so bloody bright red she looks as if she had just finished feeding off a freshly killed antelope. *This* is the New York woman, and if I have treated her kindly, forgive me—I am a gentle person.

Actually, my love affair with New York ended long ago. But I remember when I was young, I used to have a tiny room at the Claridge Hotel, which is still there. I used to look down from my window at the bright lights of Times Square and thought that it was the most magical place on our planet. And maybe it was then. Part of the fascination of everything then was the entrance to a little radio studio, right across the hall from my room. It wasn't a clandestine station, but the way it was operated made it look that way. Everybody who came and went into that studio looked like Sacco and Vanzetti. Maybe they were. I was too shy to ask.

All the great Broadway nightclubs are now just a bitter-sweet memory—killed by the repeal of Prohibition and the dirty Off-Broadway shows. And what can a dirty Off-Broadway show do onstage that can't be done better at home? In bed. And cheaper. And you don't have to try and find a taxicab afterward—unless you're a bigamist. Or a showoff.

The Broadway area seems to have become a corral for cretins. They're all penned up there together—doing their thing, which seems to consist mostly of males and females wearing each other's clothes and successfully avoiding soap and water and grade-school education. The only theaters actually on Broadway are movie theaters which are devoted to football-field-sized signs picturing Mount Everest bosoms, which even Edmund Hillary would have difficulty ascending (they look slippery). There is one fascinating sign which blows a large puff of steam from a blowhole and which has been, alternately, down through the years, the puff of a huge cigarette, the steam of a mammoth steam iron, and, more recently, a 50-foot giant with bad breath.

My stay at the St. Regal Hotel ended not with a whimper, but with a shout—when I saw the $3.48 room service had charged me for a cup of beef broth.

When I asked for an explanation, they hung me by my thumbs until I apologized for my gaucherie.

That is in the past now, but I still remember the conversation I had with one of the most famous of our theatrical female stars, who had outsmarted at least six husbands and who was appearing on the *Today* show that same morning. I had just told her my intention of living soon in the Canadian bush country.

"How could you possibly *stand* it way back there in the woods away from *everything?*" Then she lit a cigarette with trembling hands, as she looked at me, sympathetically, through her bloodshot eyes. "It's so *lonely!*"

I asked her where *she* lived.

"The St. Regal Hotel."

"Isn't it lonely *there?*" I said.

"How could it be?" She almost laughed at my naïveté. "All I have to do is pick up the phone and call room service."

Taking yourself out of the mainstream of life and up a small tributary is a good way of finding out who your friends are—not that I didn't know already, but this is a kind of test of fire for anyone with the slightest tendency to panic when he is out of sight of anything reassuring, like the Old New Litchridge Medical Center and Liquor Store. We didn't lose any friends by our retreat to nowhere, and that's the way I thought it would be.

As I write this, the temperature outside is 43 degrees below zero. A blizzard is howling down on us from the north. The antenna for our radiotelephone has been blown from its tower. We are miles and miles from any outside help if the need should arise. Am I afraid, Mr. Emerson? Yes. Will I leave here? No, Mr. Emerson. No.

7

AFTER a few soggy and scary trips on the bush road and the timber road which connected Lost Lake with Highway 365, we decided we needed something a little more swamp-worthy than our 1960 Land Rover, so again I contacted my friend in Valcourt, Quebec, Jean-Luc Bombardier. It just so happened that the Bombardier Company made a vehicle which could negotiate any terrain, had an enclosed, heated cab for three people, and could zip along at 25 miles per hour. This sounded too good to be true, but the machine, which cost more than a fancy U.S. "Soul" Cadillac with a Hammond Organ klaxon, had to give us more than the Land Rover, which wasn't too reliable in the Canadian counterpart of the Everglades—its gallant four cylinders had a tendency to gurgle "Nearer My God to Thee" as they sank beneath the waves. This happened with tiresome regularity, because we had to cross several small streams, a large creek, and a swamp to get from nowhere to somewhere. The streams had never been bridged, but the Department of Lands and Forests had laid large galvanized-iron culvert pipes in the centers of these difficult places, which really didn't help much. The streams and the creek ignored the culverts completely and just made new channels on each side of them. What they are expected to accomplish we have never learned. Except that they created a hurdle where none had existed before, and any hope of bringing in a load of undamaged bottled goods on this road was merely an impossible dream. Rolling up, up, and over and crashing down, down, and down the other side of the first culvert would create an amusing assortment of broken glass and a heady aroma of scotch, bourbon, rum, gin, muscatel, ketchup, kosher pickles, and varnish remover. The inside of the Land Rover would smell like a one-room apartment the morning after a Polish wedding. Or the morning before. Or during.

Just when we were about to forgo wine, ketchup, and other liquids, the Bombardier J-5 arrived. That was the name of our savior, J-5, without whom we might be doomed to drinking lake water exclusively and putting Mary Baker Eddy ketchup on our hamburgers. Trying to be witty, when Bobby asked what the J was for, I said, "Jesus," and from that day forward he called it the Jesus-5. Guests were visibly startled when Bobby suggested, "Papa—let's take the Jesus-five and look for a moose." Then I'd have to say, "No—the Jesus-five will scare the moose." Then the guests would say, "We have to leave now."

When I say that the J-5 arrived, I don't mean at Lost Lake. Through careful planning (logistics-wise) we had arranged for the machine to be brought north by truck and delivered at a forest rendezvous about 20 miles from camp. Unfortunately the delivery date fell on a Saturday, and our mother's little helper (Jake) was in town—under a barstool, I imagined, but I was wrong. When I called him at his home, he answered the phone. He was vague, but he answered and seemed to understand. Yes, he would drive the Rover which, of course, he had with him, and pick us up at the north end of the lake and drive us to the designated delivery place.

That night, after waiting from noon till six at the north end of the lake, Reiko, Bobby, and I boated back to camp and called again.

"Jake," I said, after he had answered on the thirty-first ring, "what the hell happened?"

"About what?" he said.

"About what!" I yelled. "You were supposed to pick us up at the north end of the lake and drive us to get the J-five!"

Quick as a flash he said, "My car is in the shop. They were supposed to call me."

I said, "What has *your* car to do with it? You know damn well you couldn't drive that timber road in your car! Why didn't you pick us up with the Rover?"

"Yeah," he said, "I guess I coulda done that." The spaces between his words grew longer and longer, and he sounded like he was doing push-ups at the same time.

"Jake. Are you all right?"

There was a long pause.

"Who's this?" he said.

"It's the voice of doom," I said.

"Oh," he said. "How did you know I was here?"

"Look," I said, "the J-five was supposed to be delivered where the Solomon timber road crosses the Duchesne timber road, and we were supposed to be there to meet the truck. We have no way of getting there unless you pick us up with the Rover!"

"I'm just leaving," he said. "I'll call you in an hour." Then he hung up.

By 10 P.M. I was desperate. I knew that the truck driver, whose name was John something or other, would have given up and left the bush for the nearest motel, so I called the salesman for Bombardier in Toronto. I had his home phone, which I considered a lucky break, until somebody picked up the phone. I said, "Is Jim Cummins there?"

"He's *never* here!" some flaming creature said, and hung up.

I called back. "Look," I said when the same voice answered, "I'm desperate."

"You're desperate!" said the thing, and hung up again. I waited for an hour and called again. The same voice answered.

I said, giving him all the benefit, "Are you the gentleman I talked to before?"

It said, *"I'm* a gentleman, but God knows what you are! And stop calling! I'm doing my nails!"

I knew then I had to find John, the truck driver, before he hauled the J-5 all the way back to Quebec, so I started calling all the nearest motels along Route 96. I was in trouble from the first call. Have you ever tried calling a motel and saying, "Is John there?" Then they say, if they answer you at all, "John who?" Then I say, "I don't know his last name, but he's driving a big truck, with a J-five on the back of it." Then they say, "J-five? Pretty short license number." Then you have to explain that J-5 isn't a license number. It's a machine that will go through swamps. Of course, then they want to know, if they have any curiosity at all, why you want to go through swamps. Then you have to tell them you have to go through swamps to get home. Then you hang up just before they're able to trace the call. We never found John. The Ontario Provincial Police, the Mounties, and the Boy Scouts of Canada did their best, but John had vanished from the face of the earth—along with our J-5. That's what we thought until the next day, when we were flying over the spot where we were to rendezvous with him, and there nestled in a clearing surrounded by thick groupings of white and red pines was our lovely new yellow J-5. Now all we had to do was get to it.

I called Jake, as much as I hated to disturb his Sunday morning hangover, and told him to drive the Rover to the Canada Goose Airways airport. For some mysterious reason, he complied. We then drove north without Jake on Highway 96 until we got to the secondary road which led to Mr. Duchesne's timber road. Mr. Duchesne's timber road was, if anything, more bumpy than it had ever been. Bobby cried all the way, and Reiko, being Japanese, didn't cry, but I knew from the patient look on her lovely face that she was planning on a mail-order hari-kiri knife for the next trip. Finally, after many air pockets and slimy skids and near-misses with partridge, grouse, and a few red squirrels we arrived at the clearing where the J-5 stood in all its shining newness. The doors were locked, so I started looking for the keys.

Forty-five minutes later I was still looking for them, and Bobby was still crying, and Reiko had abandoned the hari-kiri knife idea and was searching for a sharp stick. The J-5 is constructed like a tractor with a cab on it. The engine is in the back, for greater power, and there are very few places to hide the keys. I finally gave up.

"Screw it," I said. "Let's get in the Rover and get the hell out of here. I can't find the keys anywhere."

Bobby started crying louder and a few tones higher. He wanted to ride the J-5 and couldn't understand why adults gave up so quick on everything.

We drove the Rover back over the culvert obstacle course to the north edge of Lost Lake and thence by boat to our woodland home. Chibi, Tanuki, our other wolves, Doggie, and Pussycat were very glad to see us, even if we didn't bring a J-5 as promised.

That night, which was still Sunday, I discovered from the notches in my Indian wooden calendar, and also from a tiny page under the nude from Sam-Jack's Texaco station in Blue Mountain, I decided to try my luck again and call the salesman in Toronto, praying that someone besides Miss Tantrum of 1968 would answer the phone. St. Jude must have been listening to someone else besides Danny Thomas, because my prayers were answered, and the landlady knew immediately who I was and what my problem had become. She told me that John had called and told her that the keys were under the battery case, which was located on the back of the J-5, right over the engine and that the cover of the battery case "just lifted off." I had tried this, and the cover had not "just lifted off," but I was so grateful to talk to someone besides the queen mother I thanked the landlady profusely, promised her one of my books, and hung up.

The next morning, just when Jake was due back to work, we once again took off by boat for the north end of the lake and the Rover. The lake was socked in by a very dense fog, and as soon as we left the dock, I regretted not having left a paper trail. We did not have a compass, as who would for a three-mile daylight trip across a lake I knew like the back of my hand? I looked at the back of my hand. It didn't look too familiar. After what seemed like hours, and it was, we sighted no land or landmark. I never realized that one fog looks just like every other fog and every water looks just like every other water.

"Maybe we ought to start yelling," Reiko said.

"Yeah—the Lord's Prayer," I said.

"What's that?" said Reiko.

"It's all we Christians have in place of Buddha."

"Oh," said Reiko. "Maybe I should pray—to Buddha."

"Why don't you?" I said.

"I need drums," said Reiko.

"I gotta teach you the Lord's Prayer," I said.

"I know the Lord's Prayer," said Bobby, and started singing "My Country 'Tis of Thee" just as we hit a rock.

I shut off the motor and waited until the fog lifted. We sat there for two hours playing a game, "How to Kill Jake the Slowest Way," which Mattel has now made into a Christmas item for children who have not yet learned violence.

When we finally reached the J-5, I had no trouble at all in prying the battery cover loose and finding the keys underneath. By this time, I felt like at last we had caught up with the Holy Grail. I didn't try to explain Holy Grail to Reiko. I had spent six years trying to get through to her with immaculate conception.

Unlocking the Holy Grail, my hands were trembling like a dirty old man unbuttoning Mia Farrow. Or a dirty Mia Farrow unbuttoning an old man. But at last I was inside the cab. There were three seats—one for the driver, in the center, and two chairs, one on either side, mounted on extremely bouncy springs. Looking at the forest of control levers, I was nonplussed. I knew I could never drive this machine without a four-year course at MIT. It wasn't the plenitude of controls that made me lose all sense of adventure, but the look of cold, demoniacal polished efficiency, which seemed to say, "Only a stainless-steel super-being may operate me." I hadn't been briefed, as I was supposed to have been, if we had only met John when we were supposed to, and I knew I couldn't rely on any mechanical sense of my own; although I had spent a few years of my life driving high-powered race cars, this machine seemed a lot more dangerous. I was afraid if I pressed the wrong button or pulled the wrong lever, it would rear up and start thrashing around the bush like a wounded Jackie Gleason, destroying everything in its path.

Just when I was about to quit and leave with my tail between my legs, I found a large, thick instruction manual. I was saved. I was very good at following instructions. The instruction manual was beautifully bound, and after duly admiring its cover, I opened it to page one and read: *"Vous avez maintenant, à votre service, un tracteur à chenilles d'une conception spéciale, construit pour le plus grand nombre d'usages possible dans les conditions d'opération les plus variées."* The whole goddamn instruction book was in *French!*

8

BY the time I received the English instruction book from Mr.
Bombardier I was driving the J-5 pretty well—and the manu-
facturer was right—this machine would go anywhere that a
jeep would fear to tread. It was marvelous, although it didn't
ride any better than the Land Rover on rough ground. I
began studying truss ads, and I lost three fillings on one ride
to Loon Lake. Gradually I became used to its little quirks.
Most of the time when a small tree would get in its way, it
would just ride right over it, but occasionally we'd meet a
tree made of sterner stuff; the J-5 would bump the tree, then
proceed to climb right up the side of it. It always happened
so fast that suddenly Bobby, Reiko, and I would find ourselves seated flat on our backs like astronauts waiting for
the countdown.

Jake didn't approve of the J-5 at all, principally because I
wouldn't let him drive it. And also because I gently chided
him for not making the bush road wide enough in a few
places. I didn't want to *gently* chide him when, on the first
trip down this engineering marvel, the machine became
jammed in between a larch and a birch. I wanted to castrate
him and run his balls up on a flagpole to see if anyone would
salute them. Besides Jake.

There were other problems with Jake, which seemed to
arise with each morning's sun. According to Mr. Albert, the
former owner, Jake was an animal lover and never killed
anything except one moose once a year, for meat, which he
shared with his poor widowed sister and her thirteen children.
I'm sure that this was the impression that Jake wanted to give
Mr. Albert because Mr. Albert belonged to the Audubon

Society, but in real life, as Bluebeard used to say, things were a bit different. Everything came out in the many quiet conversations Jake and I used to have each morning, while he was steeling himself against any work that might need to be done.

"Killed a moose," Jake said, between gallbladder attacks and a racking cough which he was able to turn on and off at will, "right in the back of your office. Last winter."

"Takes a lot of guts to kill a moose," I said.

"No, it doesn't," he said. "Shot him from inside the cabin—through the window."

"Did it help?" I said. "Did you have an orgasm?"

"What's that?"

"Did you *come?*"

He immediately had a doubleheader: a gallbladder attack and racking coughing spell.

Another time, after he had finished a hard day's rest, we were talking about beavers, which were plentiful at Lost Lake and had built a tremendous dam at the other end of the lake across the creek which was the overflow from our lake and ran for a few miles to the east into Loon Lake, which emptied into McCracken Creek, thence to Blakey Creek, Bell Creek, Hope Creek, and the Parkinson River, which finally wound up boiling into North Georgian Bay. I may be telling you more than you want to know, but I have these maps, and my mother once said, "A map gets rusty if you don't use it." My mother also said, "David Merrick is not God." I don't know where she got this misinformation.

I mentioned to Jake that I had seen a particularly large beaver surface near our main island and come ashore to nibble at something on the bank.

"Have to put out some traps," he said.

"Traps?" I said. "You mean—trap the beavers?"

"Yeah," he said, plugging up his perpetual nose leak, with a soiled rag. "They'll start eating the trees."

"This one wasn't eating trees," I said. "He was eating something on the ground."

"He'll eat the trees."

"Has he ever eaten any trees before?"

"Nope."

"Then why in the hell do you say he's gonna eat the trees?"

"I know beavers," he said, losing the battle with his nose.

"Intimately?" I said.

"Huh?"

"Why don't you just put a little chicken wire around the trees nearest the water? Then no beavers can eat no trees," I said, not kindly.

"Yeah," Jake said, like a whole new world had just opened to him. "That might do it. Won't help much against flying squirrels, though."

"What?" said Bobby. "Flying squirrels! That sounds cool."

"Yeah," said Jake. "I shoot every one I see."

"Why?" Reiko said.

"They're very destructive. If they get in the house, they're murder!"

"How are they gonna get in the house?" I asked. "We gonna open the door and yell, 'Come and get it,' or something?" I found myself not too willing to suppress the killer instinct, which Margaret Mead or whoever said we all have whether we realize it or not. I realized it and I was glad. Just when I discovered we actually have flying squirrels in the neighborhood, I also learned that we have a flying squirrel assassin living with us.

"They get in," Jake said. "I kill as many as I see. And porcupines, too."

"They get in the house much?"

"No," he said. "They're mostly outside in the bush. They eat up your ax handle if you ain't watching."

"We got an ax?" I said.

"Yeah."

"Do you ever use it?"

"Well—"

"I know why porcupines eat up ax handles," Bobby said.

"So do I," Reiko said. "It's the salt on them. People sweat when they use the ax and salt gets on the handle."

"Well, I guess our ax is safe then," I said, looking right at Jake.

"Cool," said Bobby.

"I need an Alka-Seltzer," Jake said, struggling up out of our only easy chair, and shuffled out the door and down the path, which led to the footbridge to the mainland and the safety of his eighty-proof cabin. I wondered if this kindly soul had killed any of the buffalo which roamed our forest. These buffalo had long ago escaped from an experimental farm and had impudently returned to the wild, where they conducted their *own* experiments and were multiplying rapidly.

The next time Jake took off for the fleshpots of Chinook-ville, I threw all his rusty traps into the deepest part of the lake, and after hours of tedious gunsmithing, I fixed the trigger on his rifle so it just hung there like that little thing that hangs down in the back of your throat. Then I wrote every animal dealer I know in hopes that I might pick up a cheap grizzly and let him loose near Jake's cabin. This will make a marvelous home movie for the Griffin show.

9

READING matter at Lost Lake is a problem. I mean current reading matter. On this particular bright, foggy summer's morning because of a habit which I well established back in Old New Litchridge I was sipping my instant coffee and enjoying the New York *Daily News*. The December 26, 1968, three-star edition. I was enjoying it because I hadn't read it before. I had found it wrapped around an old Lynbrook High School basketball trophy, which was a sort of mystery trophy because I had no idea where it came from. I had never played with anything *round* in my whole life.

Although the *Daily News* was months old, it contained a marvelous Christmas story by-lined Dennis Eskow:

Seven men and three women celebrating Christmas in a ginmill laughed themselves sick early yesterday when a patron mistakenly put 55 cents into a jukebox instead of a cigaret machine.

"I didn't want 'Rudolph the Red-Nosed Reindeer,' I wanted a pack of Camels," the man said. He said it again and the more he said it, the heartier the other customers laughed. They laughed until they cried.

The man who wanted the cigarets stormed out. He returned in 15 minutes with a .38 caliber revolver. He pointed the gun in the general direction of the bar and squeezed the trigger. Five men were wounded, one critically.

It was a perfect Christmas story, but it depressed me. Maybe we *didn't* belong out in the wild Canadian bush. Maybe we were missing all the *fun*.

"Reiko!" I yelled toward our cavernous kitchen. "Let's go to Chinookville!"

She came into the living room, her face blanched. "I don't want to go to Chinookville. Please don't make me!"

I understood her concern. The trip from our island to Chinookville was something Lewis and Clark would have thought twice about—and Neil Armstrong would have been court-martialed for refusing altogether.

"Look, Cho-cho-san," I said. "Lieutenant Pinkerton wants to go to Chinookville—that's an order!"

"I'm going back Japan," she said, and ran to the bedroom and started throwing kimonos into a suitcase.

"I thought you said Japan was too damn crowded now," I said, handing her an obi (a stuffed pillow with brocade ribbons Japanese girls wear, resting on their tiny butts, which makes them look like a combination pincushion and tea cozy).

"I'm going back Japan," Reiko repeated, trying to jam a pair of long Ojibway snowshoes into her too-short suitcase.

"What are you packing those for?" I said.

"Souvenir of Canada—for my father," she said.

"Do you think he'll be able to ride his bicycle with those things on?" She gave up on the snowshoes and tried a pair of deer-foot gun racks instead. They didn't make it either.

"Look," I said, "even if you go back Japan, you'll have to go Chinookville first."

"I'll fly there. Call Canada Goose," she said.

"I did call," I said. "It's too misty; the ceiling is too low. They'd never be able to find Lost Lake."

"We're really lost, aren't we?" she said.

"Oh, for godsakes," I said. "That's what you liked about it. What happened?"

"That road to Chinookville. Those big holes and those big tin pipes—and that swamp! Every time we cross that swamp I get very scared. We almost get stuck every time."

"Almost doesn't count," I said.

"What's that mean?" she said.

"I don't know," I said. "Come on—let's go to Chinookville. Who knows? The road may be better now. The Department of Lands and Forests promised—sort of—that they'd work on it—someday."

She didn't say anything, but she stopped packing. I called to Bobby. "Bobby, put your shoes on—we're going to Chinookville!"

Bobby ran out of the house in his bare feet and into the woods.

After finding Bobby in the hollow of an old lightning-struck pine, we forced his shoes onto his feet and jerked the outboard motor to life and started for the north end of the lake, where our 1960 Land Rover patiently waited for us to try and start her.

The fog was beginning to burn off the lake, and here and there we could see patches of the brilliant blue Canadian sky. I know the sky is blue everywhere, but here it's a special blue like it was arranged by the Chinookville Chamber of Commerce—in tune with their summertime campaign on the Chinookville television station which has hundreds of spot announcements, sprinkled through the latest 1927 movies, which read "Welcome to Our American Visitors." This was only during the summer, when they *have* American visitors. During the other three seasons it was a tacit "What the hell are you doin' here at this time of the year?"

During the voyage to the north end we saw the three loons who inhabit our lake. This is all we ever saw—just three. We were even thinking of changing the name to Three Loon Lake (which has sort of a double meaning), but suddenly a fourth loon showed up and spoiled everything. But loons are great to watch because they rarely fly. Their specialty is diving for fish or just diving to get out of the way of our boat. After they dive, they seem to be down forever; then they come up a couple of hundred yards away and always in a different direction from which they dived. And their wonderfully weird cries are difficult to describe, because they actually have so many types. I think the one we all love best on a very still evening—usually just after the sun has set and the western skies are shot with colors that don't even exist—is when the loon lets go with a wild, quavering shriek which sounds exactly like a woman in labor or a hot grandmother being attacked by a sex maniac. Or both. It *is* wild and wonderful, and I think if I can hear this sound on my deathbed, it will be all the exit music I'll ever need.

As our little Springbok boat pushed through the blue-green water, the noise disturbed an occasional raven, which roosts only in the tallest pines. The raven looks like a humpbacked crow, but much bigger. Black ducks skimmed the water, flying at a tremendous speed, and terns wheeled and dived for their breakfasts. The fog was almost all burned off as we approached the huge beaver dam that plugged the little creek. This was the beaver dam that Jake dynamited occasionally to keep the water in the lake from "getting too high." Anyway, this was his story, and on these expeditions to wreak havoc with the eager beavers' handiwork, we never heard the sound of dynamite exploding. When I asked him about this, he said he stuck the explosive deep in the mud and it muffled the sound. A likely story. Nothing could muffle the sound on that rock-ribbed lake. Later on, after Jake had been dismissed from our employ, we never interfered with the dam with dynamite or anything else and the water in the lake remained at a constant level. This was just another one of Jake's ploys to avoid irritating his muscles by using them for anything other than holding a bottle or a lurid paperback. And that's something else—he used to grab *my* lurid paperbacks before I was finished with them. Many's the time I never did find out whether the beautiful love-starved schoolteacher and her precocious and overdeveloped teen-age daughter were raped by the overdeveloped, love-starved coal miner in shaft number nine, where he had chained them, nude and screaming. I figured they *were*, because when you are a love-starved schoolteacher and a precocious, overdeveloped teen-ager chained nude in a coal mine by an overdeveloped, love-starved coal miner, a mile and a half below Scranton, Pennsylvania, things *could* happen. After all, this *is* still the land of opportunity. If you know where to look.

When we arrived at the beaver dam, the beavers were apparently taking five because there wasn't one in sight, and from the looks of their project, it would take a direct hit from a multiple megaton bomb to jar it loose. Not that this would dissuade any right-thinking beaver for one moment. As soon as the dust had settled, they'd be right back on the job and in twenty-four hours or less there would be a brand-new, fully completed dam. Beavers have the same boundless energy and initiative and enthusiasm for their work that the average American housemaid had. In 1906.

We had a little wooden dock next to the beaver dam, and after hitting a few submerged rocks in the narrow channel, with the usual accompaniment of much Japanese advice on how to steer a boat from Reiko and stream of updated ancient marine curses from me, while Bobby sang "Old Macdonald had a farm and on that farm he had some labor trouble" softly to himself, I managed to steer the Springbok head on into the front of the dock, throwing everybody violently to the wet floor. I always seemed to forget which way to twist the tiller (which was also the accelerator) to the "off" position. The front end of the boat or *bow* (according to Coast Guard navigation terminology), because of these many unorthodox landings, looks like Tony Galento.

"You don't know anything about steering a boat," Reiko said.

"There's too goddamn many rocks around here," I said. "Why the hell did that idiot Jake have to build the dock here?"

"There are rocks everywhere in this lake," Reiko said. "This lake is a glacial lake. It was formed by the last great glacier—about twelve thousand years ago. That's why it's full of rocks. The glacier just melted and left them here."

I couldn't believe what I was hearing. Reiko, so far as I knew, was entirely ignorant of anything remotely connected with geology. Now here she was spouting off about glaciers. She even knew the date. "Where the hell did you get that information?" I said.

"From the *Reader's Digest*." (John Reddy of the *Digest* had arranged for Reiko to receive the Japanese edition every month.)

"Oh," I said, not quite sure that John Reddy had done me a favor or not. Supposing she read something in there about women's suffrage—or money or Hugh O'Brian? Or better yet or worse still—George Hamilton?

"Next time," Reiko said, *"I* steer the boat to the dock."

"If we ever get a sampan, you can steer, okay?" I said.

"That's Chinese," Reiko said. "A sampan."

"Yeah," said Bobby, "sampan."

"You keep out of this!" I said.

"Stop yelling!" Reiko yelled.

"Wanna scare the buffalo?" Bobby said.

We tied the boat up at the dock and unloaded our survival devices for the trip down the timber road to the highway. The survival devices didn't consist of much at that time of year. A few bottles of Coke for Dad, and some inflated rubber cushions and many straps and belts for Reiko and Bobby. We also carried a small chain saw, a hand winch with 50 feet of thin, very strong steel cable, shovels, picks, chains, and a small box of smoke flares, which, if in case of our getting stranded in the bush, would bring the Department of Lands and Forests plane in five minutes. Theoretically.

After we had loaded the Land Rover, I connected the two cables which had been previously removed from the battery and stepped on the starter. It was a holy day. She started. We all took one last look back at the lake, which was so smooth and beautiful and so easy to travel on. Sadly I put the Rover into low-low second gear and off we lurched into the Valley of Death—without the 600. There was just us, and 12 miles of swamp, rock, tree stumps, bottomless potholes, unburied steel conduit pipe, greasy mud, and fallen trees.

The Rover pitched so hard at the first pothole, which was Grand Canyonesque, the spare tire, so picturesquely attached to the engine hood, like those African safari outfits, broke loose and rolled down a very ambitious creek. I say "ambitious," because for a creek this size it was sure trying to cover a lot of territory. The tire remained upright and rolling—flinging itself high into the air with every rock it hit, and coming down again—rolling on and on, until it finally smashed into a massive granite outcropping, with a lovely razor-sharp gneiss shard at just the right level to slice an eight-inch hole in the heavy tread. My diagnosis: The gash was terminal.

The tire didn't roll through the creek so easily on the way back. It was like trying to push a lesbian salmon upstream to spawn. Several times I was tempted to abandon it to its fate, but on thinking about it, maybe a replacement for a Land Rover tire and wheel might not be so standard an item in Chinookville. Although it was an up-and-coming little town like Point Barrow, there were some things, such as frozen TV dinners and butter knives, which they had never heard of. Apparently. On second thought, they *did* have frozen TV dinners, but it wasn't intentional.

After a terrific fight and tearing my only pair of *town* corduroy pants on another handy gneiss shard (no doubt about it—we were in the handy gneiss shard country), I reached the immobile Land Rover and hoisted the spare wheel and its useless tire into the back. From the looks on my Ming Toy wife and her kid I didn't think it would be right if I searched the surrounding bush for the missing nut that had held the wheel on the hood. The Rover didn't look so safari-ish now, but at least we knew where the spare wheel was.

"Everybody set to go to town?" I said, with a merry twinkle as I shifted our sturdy vehicle back into low-low second gear.

Reiko didn't say anything, but Bobby said, "I wish *I* had a tire to chase."

We moved downhill toward the first swamp, where usually we would see a moose or two standing belly-deep in the water and waiting for us to get the hell out of there so they could finish eating without the accompaniment of an overheated Rover in low-low second. Today, as we smashed from side to side inside the cab of the Rover and rolled over rock and root and what felt like abandoned mine shafts, we saw no moose. It was going to be one of those days. Seeing a moose or elk or some other animal on that road somehow made the bone-crushing ride somewhat less like an Aztec human sacrifice and more like an Apache puberty rite. Which, I'm told, really smarts—if you're a pube.

The second trial we found ourselves facing after a couple of miles of dune buggy broncobusting was an engine that suddenly started the Old Faithful bit; only our little Rover was shooting that hot steam a helluva lot higher than the one those Yellowstone folks have. She needed water and badly, but naturally it was the old story—after oozing through swamps and fording the wildest of rampant creeks, we now found ourselves on the surface of the moon. In the loneliest, remotest, and driest spot for 10,000 miles. This situation was to test my every "survival in the wilds" knowledge. I thought —now if this was the Arizona desert, I could tap a barrel cactus and get all the water we needed and still have some left over to mix us up a batch of Tang. But this wasn't the Arizona desert. This was the dry part of Canada. The driest of the dry parts of Canada. The spot in which our only link with civilization chose to become arid apparently had never seen any kind of precipitation or ground moisture.

There was only one thing to do. I sacrificed my precious supply of Coca-Cola. This helped some, but not enough, so we each—Reiko, Bobby, and myself—took two empty Coke bottles and started searching for anything liquid.

As we trudged down the timber road for what seemed like miles, Bobby kept asking questions. "Where are we going, Papa?"

"We're looking for water," I said.

"I want apple juice," Bobby said.

"If we had apple juice, we'd put it in the car," I said.

"Does the car like apple juice?"

"I don't care whether it does or not," I said.

"Don't you like cars, Papa?" Bobby said.

"I love cars," I said. "That's why we have to find some water. I want to give our car a drink."

"Does our car like water better than apple juice?" Bobby said.

"When we get back, why don't you ask it?" I said.

"Cars can't talk," Reiko said.

"How do you know?" I said. "You've been in Japan all your life."

"I had to be in Japan," Reiko said.

"I know why," said Bobby. "Because you're Japanese."

"Bobby," I said, "you're the smartest kid in a hundred miles."

"I am?" said Bobby.

Being an ideal father, I didn't tell him he was the *only* kid in a hundred miles. The rest were squirrels.

After filling our Coke bottles at the nearest bubbling brook, we walked back to the Rover and poured the precious stuff into its radiator. It wanted more. A lot more. Five more trips to the bubbling brook more. Then it was sated, surfeited, and overflowing. Vowing on the grave of my mother to buy a large tank with extra water, I slipped, jerked, forced, and ground the car's guts back into low-low second gear and away we plunged toward the halfway point between Lost Lake and the highway—the "Great Swamp."

The Great Swamp had been bridged a few years before by the Department of Lands and Forests with a very nervous causeway of what seemed to be the most treacherous species of quicksand, which had been sold to them as gravel. Gravel being a very scarce commodity up there on the Cambrian Shield, which translated to layman's language (which is all we have) means solid rock from the Great Lakes to the Arctic Ocean.

To negotiate the Great Swamp stretch, you have to throw the Rover into low-low-*low third* gear, shove the gas pedal through the floorboards and pray loud and clear, because if you stop anywhere in this quaking trap, you are there from now on. A winch will do you no good, because after you attach it to your car, what else is there to attach the other end to? Nothing. There's not a tree within a thousand feet of this sandy tightrope. So far, in our year and a half of hell-driver practice on this Canadian Burma Road, we have successfully raced across this spot—but almost never in a straight line. It's impossible to drive across this whispering, shifting, slithering mess without making most of the trip at right angles with the road. I know that if I hadn't been well schooled in driving on slick pavements in all kinds of weather in my race-driving days, I never would have been able to stay on this sandy causeway from one end to the other. It was seat-of-the-pants driving at its ultimate.

Once again, we crossed this super-obstacle successfully, with very little internal bleeding. From the Great Swamp to the highway was easy sledding, as the cliché goes. Preferably with a sled, but with the Land Rover, it wasn't really too bad. There were a few air pockets, at which point everything, tools, spare tire, empty Coke bottles, and the Swiss Family Douglas would crash against the top of the Rover with a splintering crunch, followed by vows from Reiko and echoes from Bobby that they would never travel this road again. Never.

"This isn't as bad as the subway in New York," I consoled

them. "At least here you aren't gonna get the bubonic plague or mugged. Or both."

"I wanna ride the subway when we get to Chinookville," Bobby said.

"Okay," I said, "you ride the subway, and I'll ride the big pink clam or whatever it was with Dr. Dolittle down the Chinook River."

"I wanna ride the pink clam," Bobby said.

"With Dr. Dolittle?" I said.

"Who's he?" Bobby said, proving once again that he was the smartest kid in a hundred miles—or maybe more.

Despite the series of near disasters and breaking of all of the Rover's springs, we finally arrived at the little lumber camp which was halfway from the halfway point to the highway. When I say little "lumber camp," I'm exaggerating. I'm stretching. It's an old show biz characteristic—forgive me. This lumber camp consisted of one shanty with burlap roof and walls housing two superhardy souls who worked from before sunrise to long after sundown. They had three machines to help them. One to push down the trees (they never *cut* them down), one "grabber" I called it, which grabbed up a stack of logs and piled them on a truck that looked like World War I war surplus. They also had a chain saw which cut the wood to six-foot lengths, which seemed to be standard for wood destined for the pulp mill. And to the pulp mill is where they drove their vintage carrier every night after dark with its overload. The pulp mill was a good 75 or 80 miles from where they were lumbering, so it's doubtful that they ever slept. There couldn't have been any time for such frivolity.

Sunday was no day of rest for these two. They spent the day sharpening the chain saw and stapling their truck back together. They had a little boy, who disappeared in the fall. I presumed that his fun days of sitting around on a rock all day, watching his dad and his uncle (if that's who they were) knock down trees and sharpen saws, were over and he was back in school.

I must be vague about the two lumberjacks because these two sweat-soaked, begrimed tillers of the forest would never stop work long enough to talk to us. They must have set up an impossible quota of pulp logs per day, or else they had enormous life insurance policies and were trying for heart attacks. I was all for taking a couple of policies on them myself. At the rate these two were going, I could see me as an overnight *nouveau riche,* having the last laugh on Equitable Life, while their frantic actuaries spent the next twenty years trying to find out what went wrong with their foolproof system.

About the only information I learned about these two was that they were not French. I found that out when I asked them to translate the French Bombardier instruction book for the Jesus-5. They denied being French so vehemently I feared I had committed some sort of etiquette breach, and to compound the mystery about the two hardest-working mortals I have ever observed, I have not learned after almost a year and a half why they were so bruised by my inquiry. Maybe they *are* French and can't read. That could be it. Those French verbs could have been too much for them.

Besides being the most dedicated workers in the world, they must be the hardiest of humans. The flimsy half tent they slept in was made from gossamer burlap, which was patched with flattened sections of rusty gasoline tins. I haven't the slightest idea of how they attached the tin to the burlap and vice versa, but they managed. At best this poor-white wigwam wouldn't keep out the springtime blackfly plague and in the dead of winter I'm sure they would have been much warmer at bedtime if they had lain down in the middle of the road and covered themselves with rose petals and concentrated on one-fourth of Sophia Loren. Or on real cold nights—one-half.

But enough of the Frick and Frack of the north woods, we were on our way to Chinookville, the fun city of the Arctic Circle set. Remember?

After passing the lumber camp, the road lost most of its adventure. It was almost smooth. Like the surface of an uninhabited planet. We breezed along at 25 miles an hour, despite the hernia which one of the front tires had developed back there where things weren't so good. The highlight of this final few miles before we reached the highway was the advent of the nutty wolf. He must have been a little off his rocker, because I have never seen a wolf act as he did, nor have I ever met anyone who has. This huge male wolf suddenly appeared on the road in front of the Rover and ran in front of us for a mile or so, and when we had to slow down for a creeklet or a tree partially blocking the road, this lovely animal would slow down and wait for us. Looking over his shoulder all the while. We couldn't believe it.

"What's he trying to prove?" I said. "He should dive into the bush and hide until we predators have passed by. He's not going to last long with these kinds of tactics if he tries them with somebody else."

"What's that mean?" said Reiko.

"In Ontario," I said, "the government pays money if you kill a wolf."

"Why?" Bobby said.

"Because somebody up there read 'Little Red Riding Hood' and believed every word of it."

"Sonsabitches!" Bobby sagely said.

"We're almost to the highway," Reiko said.

"Oh—yes," I said. At that moment the wolf, which also knew we were near the highway, leaped over a huge, rotting log and disappeared into the dense forest at the side of the road. I would like to say here that not once during his playful escapade of leading us down this woodland garden path did he skulk. Every description of a wolf and its actions has him skulking or sneaking or cowering or slinking. Wolves never skulk or slink, except when sniffing the ground. It is very difficult *not* to skulk or slink when ground sniffing—unless you're an anteater. Or Barbra Streisand.

Highway 365, such as it is, was a welcome sight, and the only hazard it had to offer, outside of a few one-way bridges, was bear droppings. I don't know why, but this seemed to be a favorite place for evacuation. I guess the bears are entitled to this little idiosyncrasy. If elephants have a favorite Forest Lawn where they go to die, why can't the bears have a favorite place to shit? I must ask Dr. Brothers.

Highway 365 led us after 10 miles to another highway. This one is the direct route to Chinookville, which was a mere 96 miles away. This route wasn't particularly scenic, but we did pass through the village of Chapeau, which was named after Pierre Le Chapeau, who, legend tells us, was shot through the hat by an Iroquois arrow way back in 1786. Legend also tells us that the arrow also went through Pierre Le Chapeau's head, which cut short his beaver-trapping career. Pierre Le Chapeau had founded this village named after him just the year before that and he lived just long enough to see three houses spring up almost overnight. The three houses are still there and they are now filling stations. Also that is the extent of the building boom started by Pierre Le Chapeau, with the exception of a brand-new modern school on a slight rise above the village.

I was thrilled when I first saw this school and I asked at one of the filling stations about it.

"Oh," the filling station boy said, worrying his acne while filling my tank, "that school is closed. The kids now go to school up to Wally Lake. Up the road."

"How far up the road?" I said.

"Can't be more'n eighty, ninety miles," the acne king said, switching his activities from his face to his rear end, which apparently was badly in need of succor.

"What's happening with the school up there?" I said, indicating the new building on a nearby hill.

"Oh," he said, "it's now a community center."

I paused for a few moments, while he serviced his rear end, his face, and a new area—his crotch. Then I said, "How many people in this village?"

"Well," he said, "since Old Man Tilburg died, we got about five."

"And that's the community center up there?" I said.

"Yeah."

"Must be great on long winter evenings," I said.

"No fun," he said.

"How come?" I said.

"Well, we know you live around here somewhere, so I'll tell you," he said. "Old Man Tilburg was the village drunk, and he was real entertaining—at the community center—but since he died, we just go up there on Saturday nights and watch the roof leak."

"I'm sorry to hear that Old Man Tilburg died," I said.

"Oh," he said, wiping his nose on his arm, "it's really not so bad now. That roof leaks pretty good sometimes. We've had some good Saturday nights—'specially in the spring."

"What do you do on a Saturday night when it doesn't rain?" I was foolish enough to ask.

The acne king hesitated at this, then decided that I was an OK guy who lived around there somewhere. "That's how we lost Old Man Tilburg. It was his idea, though."

"It was, huh?" I said. "What was his idea?"

"You're gonna laugh," he said.

"No, I won't," I promised.

"Well, one night, when it wasn't raining and there wasn't no leak to watch, Old Man Tilburg came up with a new game—he read about it in the *Liberty* magazine."

"*Liberty* magazine!"

"Yeah. Old Man Tilburg used to save old magazines. That was his hobby. That and guns. That's how he come to show us this new game. Russian roulette he called it."

"I know the game," I said.

"Well, anyway, Old Man Tilburg showed us how to play it—and that was it. Bam! He was dead. He didn't have a chance."

"Did he spin the cylinder before he pulled the trigger?" I said.

"What cylinder?" he said. "Old Man Tilburg used a single-shot derringer."

"Well," I said, "that's *Liberty* magazine for you—you had to read those goddamn stories so fast you sometimes missed a point or two."

"Yeah, I guess so," he said, "but now we got a better game than *Liberty* magazine. More exciting."

"How's that?" I asked.

"Well, for one thing we don't use a pistol or any kinda gun—we use bows and arrows."

"Russian roulette—with bows and arrows—that doesn't sound right," I said. "With a pistol you get more suspense. You never know what's gonna happen."

"I know," he said. "We got the same thing—only the whole game is a little more subtle and sophisticated."

I picked up my ears at this kind of talk. "Oh?" I said. "How come?"

"One of the arrows," he said, "is poisoned. Check your oil?"

10

THE rest of the trip to Chinookville was uneventful (this time) except for the insistent pounding of the herniated left front tire. The farther we got from Le Chapeau and its three filling stations, the more ominous it sounded, but we made it to Chinookville.

Chinookville is exciting—like Philadelphia or Des Moines or Fort Wayne, or maybe even Providence, Rhode Island. It has a supermarket, a television repair shop, a boutique, a *salon de beauté*, a government liquor store, and a few other facilities which enabled almost everyone in Chinookville to live just as *House Beautiful* and Amy Vanderbilt and John Lennon and Yoko say we should.

Chinookville, because of the nearby presence of mines and miners, had at least twenty dine-and-dance and juice joints, each with its own rock-and-roll group. Checking the amusement page of the Chinookville *Star*, I learned that the King George Airplane was—or were—appearing at Mammy's Chicken Shack. Fu Man and the Chus were at Schwartz's Chicken Shack. Lucky Pierre's Chicken Shack and Bit of Old Mexico was featuring Irving Alpert and his Marijuana Grass (which I thought was cute). Then there was Pussy and Her Galores direct from Paris, France—they were appearing at Prince Romanoff's Chicken Shack, Pizza Parlor, and Pissoir. I never have checked to see if this was the same Prince Romanoff, the last of the Harry Gergusons. Personally I think it is just someone who has stolen the prince's good name. The list of fun spots seemed endless and whether they were fun or not I had yet to find out. The Gay White Way of Chinookville *may* be all tinsel and punctured balloons.

Real life could be back in Chapeau—watching a leaky roof on a Saturday night. This might be what it's all about. Color television, see-through gowns, and nude-ins at senior citizen villages may not be the answer.

There was another form of entertainment, not advertised as such, in the Chinookville supermarket, where each product is labeled in both French and English—with French in bolder lettering, making it very hard for Reiko to shop. This makes for a thrilling life when you get back home, 116 miles from the supermarket, to discover that what you thought was a can of beans turns out to be tinned Brillo. Very chewy and almost devoid of vitamins. And let's face it—canned beans just will not remove coffee stains from your sink.

The ever-present unhappy vision of that horrendous road into Lost Lake always influenced the amount of our supermarket purchases. We tried to get enough so we wouldn't have to make this dire drive any oftener than we had to; consequently we overloaded the little Land Rover mercilessly. If it has shock absorbers and springs, they are anonymous, so this overloading did not noticeably disturb its Plimsoll line. Therefore, we had no way of knowing how much it would "bottom out" when we charged through an open pit on our way back home. The result of this was a blood-red trail from the highway to Lost Lake, but not from blood—mainly from pickled beets and ketchup. No matter how much cotton batting, straw, old burlap, or crumpled newspaper we wrapped around each individual bottle and jar, somehow during this incredible journey they'd shake themselves loose and smash into the ever-present chain saw or a rusty jack or sometimes the metal roof of the Rover. No matter what, we always left a trail like a wounded moose along the entire route from 365 to the lake.

We finally solved the problem of the pickled beets by crossing them off the menu, but the ketchup we felt was necessary to our sense of security and well-being, so we emptied the bottles into old Moroccan leather wine bags, which took care of the breakage problem, but ketchup out of a Moroccan wine bag never failed to shake up an honored guest who had just stopped by for a midday meal with us. Reiko *did* make rather an odd picture, standing there with a 20-gallon wine bag slung over her shoulder, asking Prince Philip if he'd care for a little ketchup on his hamburger.

Besides the food we needed, Chinookville provided us with worms to fish with. Strange, but there were no worms in the bush. It seems they like to be around where people are. Maybe that's why they're worms. Anyway, we bought our worms from our friendly BA filling station man, who kept them in a huge white refrigerator in two dozen, four dozen, or eight dozen worm containers. We could catch just as many fish with bacon rind or a bare hook for that matter, but Reiko had read something in the Japanese *Reader's Digest,* so we had to buy worms, which we kept in *our* refrigerator, which was a sure way to discourage midnight snackers. It was always a sneaky "What have we here?" followed by "Oh, my God!"

After a few more stops around town, we headed back toward the bush, and with a great feeling of relief that we were all set with the wherewithal to keep ourselves reasonably alive for the next couple of weeks.

About halfway from Chinookville to where we turn off onto Highway 365 there is something called the Washburn Industrial Farm. It is a prison, or more accurately an honor farm, where first offenders and offenders who may be considered honorable, I presume, are sent for two years, which is the maximum at this place. Long before you reach the entrance to this honor farm, there are signs warning you that it is a prison and you should not under any circumstances pick up any hitchhikers, and for a very good and obvious reason—according to the Chinookville *Star,* almost every day of the week droves of "honor" prisoners escape from this honor farm, which is kind of sad but also funny. It is easy for them to escape, because the guards do not carry weapons of any nature and also the prisoners are not incarcerated in cells or even locked buildings. They are out in the fields—tilling the soil, tending the flocks, or bringing home the cows and whatever else there is to do on a farm. This makes it very easy to escape. But—escape to *where?* If they light off into the bush, they'll never be found again till the following spring, and there won't be very much left to find. Or they can attempt to hitchhike a ride on the highway, which is equally hopeless because of the hundreds of signs warning the drivers against this. They can, of course, always arrange for someone to pick them up, but this again borders on the futile because this highway is hundreds of miles long with no side roads

going anywhere except back into the bush, and as soon as
the "honor" prisoner is found to be missing, a roadblock is
immediately set up and wham, bam, thank you, ma'am, he is
back in Washburn, where in no time he is shipped out to a
place where there is less honor and more bars.

It was along this stretch of road we had the flat tire. With
no spare, and—thanks to Jake Moon—if we had had a spare,
there were no tools anywhere aboard our sturdy little vehicle
which we could use to change over. We were stuck. Forgetting about the area we were in, I tried to flag down a car.
I have never been so *avoided* in my whole life. Cars would
skid around me on the far side of the road, then fishtail flat
out down the road and into the next county as fast as they
could. Which was plenty fast. Every time I raised my arm
to an oncoming car it was like the starting signal at a drag
strip. One gigantic tractor-trailer vehicle almost jackknifed
his whole load of nitroglycerin to pass a little old lady in
a 1912 Willys-Overland, who was going 90 after seeing me.
The driver of that rig was the most skillful I have ever seen.
How he ever got that trailer disciplined into following him
again I'll never know. The smell of burning rubber hovered
in the air for an hour.

Finally, after we had tried every ruse, including me lying
down on the pavement and having Reiko and Bobby pray
over me (nobody even slowed down), I started to walk to
the prison farm entrance.

The guards at the prison gatehouse greeted me with mixed
emotions. "My name is Jack Douglas," I said. This set the
wheels going. One clerical-type guard immediately went to a
filing cabinet, opened one of its steel drawers, and started
to shuffle the hundreds of papers enclosed within.

"I've been out on the highway, trying to get some one to
stop for me, but—" I continued, tightening the noose around
my neck. The activity in the small guardroom increased
noticeably.

"You spell your name with one *s* or two?" asked the file
clerk.

"It doesn't matter how I spell my name," I said. "Look, I
don't wanna be rude, but I gotta get outta here. My wife and
little boy are waiting for me out on the highway."

"You aren't going anywhere, Buster," said the weakest-
looking guard, who was undoubtedly the toughest.

"What about my wife and my little boy?" I said. "They're waiting for me."

"Pretty handy," said the man at the files. "One *s*, huh?"

"I didn't say that," I said. "But that's how you spell it."

"Now we're getting someplace," said the weak-looking one.

"Look," I said, "let's start over."

"That's what they all say," said a third guard, who had just come in, leading three discouraged bloodhounds, who immediately threw themselves forlornly on the floor and into a comalike sleep—kicking spasmodically—dreaming of happier days back in Mississippi.

"My name is Jack Douglas, and I write books—"

"Good," the file clerk said, with a gap-toothed giggle, "we'll getcha a pad and a nice sharp crayon."

The other two guards giggled right along with him.

"Haven't you guys ever seen me on television?" I almost screamed and at the same time almost stamped my foot. I said this with the full knowledge that we had never been on the Chinookville station, but I hoped against hope that maybe one of them had caught us in Toronto or Montreal or one of the fifty or so other Canadian stations that carried the shows we are on.

"You a hockey player?" asked the guy with the bloodhounds.

"No, and I'm not in *The Glenn Miller Story* either," I said, these being the two most outstanding features of CKCV, the voice of northern Ontario. Hockey games all week, and *The Glenn Miller Story*, with Jimmy Stewart, always seemed to be the Saturday night movie.

This kind of flip answer only tended to make my three members of the Ontario penal system rather standoffish. If not downright rude.

"Okay, Buster, now let's get this straight," said the tough weak-looking one. "You were hitchhiking down the highway —to where?"

"Lost Lake," I said.

"Hey," he said to his fellow inquisitors, "we got a smart one for a change—he really picked himself a hideout where *nobody* could find him."

"I *live* there!" I found myself yelling. "I live there with my wife and my little boy and my dogs and my cougar and my five wolves!"

This stopped everything cold. They all stood frozen. This was a story they had never heard before. Or since. Almost three minutes passed before the file clerk picked up the telephone and dialed; then keeping his eye on me, he said into the mouthpiece, "Hello, Mac—we got a junkie down here who—"

I started out the door at this and was immediately grabbed by all three. I wrenched off their clutches and said, in what I hoped was a steely voice, "You do that again and Admiral Nimitz will be firing on Fort Sumter all over again—now cool it."

This seemed to slow them down a bit, while they untangled what I had said. It slowed me down too while *I* untangled it. Then I suddenly got brilliant and said, "Look, why don't you call my lawyer in Chinookville—his name is Ike Reid—he'll tell you who I am and where I live. He'll tell you I'm not an escapee, as you guys seem to think."

"Well," said the tough weakling, "maybe we have been a little hasty in judging you, but you don't know what we go through here every day. These guys don't have any honor at *all*. We wear out five or six bloodhounds a week bringing these bums back."

"They got honor," said the file clerk. "I think it's because they don't want to be farmers. That's the way it is today— they all want to be Rock Hudson."

"Oh, come on now, Joe," said the tough weakling. "Why the hell would anybody wanna be Rock Hudson?"

"Who's Rock Hudson?" said the guy with the bloodhounds.

A half hour later, with a brand-new tire substituting for the herniated one, we were once again on our not-so-merry way. We were not so merry because we had the specter of our terrible timber road hanging over our already crumpled buttocks.

11

WHEN we left Old New Litchridge for our new home in the north, the Old New Litchridge Chamber of Commerce gave me a testimonial dinner, to which I took my own food taster, who died in agony right after the chicken à la king—just before he got to the poisoned apple pandowdy.

At this auspicious and *sus*picious occasion I was given, with much accompanying oratory, a farewell gift, which turned out, on closer inspection, to be a beautiful pair of petrified dinosaur dung cuff links. I'm sure I was visibly shaken by this token of depreciation from all those who knew and loved me in Old New Litchridge.

At first I couldn't believe my good fortune, or that the cuff links were genuinely what they were supposed to be, but the little card in the silk-lined velvet box told the whole story: "One hundred and fifty million years ago the giant dinosaurs who roamed our earth left their bones. But that was not all! Anthropologists have discovered their droppings. During the vast time span, these droppings have become petrified, like rock, and now can be found in remote corners of the world in this amazing jadelike form. Polished and mounted, they are crafted into stunning cuff links. Dinosaur droppings are scientifically named coprolite, from the Greek *kopros* (dung) and *lithos* (stone). This fossilized excrement of extinct giant lizards is a 150,000,000-year-old treasure."

Also they are just the thing to start fights in saloons. Can you imagine standing next to some stevedore in a waterfront bar, and he says, "Hey—them cuff links of yours is pretty. What are they made out of?" Then you say, "Dinosaur shit." You'd never get out of there alive.

Anyway, thank you, Old New Litchridge Chamber of Commerce. You're beautiful when you're angry.

Mr. and Mrs. Albert, who owned our magnificent little settlement before we did, didn't have any coprolite mementos distributed around the main lodge and in the little niches which were indented into the face of the huge fireplace, but they had many Indian and Eskimo artifacts, some of which they left for us to enjoy. And enjoy them we did. Especially some of the Eskimo carved walrus tusks which told a story. They were apparently dirty stories, because one walrus tusk was carved with an extremely male Eskimo being chased over an ice floe by an extremely pregnant polar bear. This was walrus tusk number two. I'd give the world to see what happened on walrus tusk number one, but I think Mrs. Albert took that one with her. She mentioned something about some things which had been in the family a long time.

The Alberts were apparently more than well-to-do, because from the evidence of 20-gallon silver coffee urns and immense cooking pots and hundreds of crystal liquor glasses, which they gave us when they left, they must have had mobs of people up during the months they stayed there during the summer. This theory of the Alberts' financial structure was further augmented by a list that Mr. Albert authored some years ago. This was a list of rules and regulations for visitors to Lost Lake and the Albert compound. I have already quoted from Rule 3 about what to do when lost in the bush, but the other suggestions I find equally as helpful and maybe interesting. Anyway, it will give a clearer picture of life under the big top of the brilliant blue of the lovely Canadian sky (when it's brilliantly blue and lovely). This is Mr. Albert's list with a few additions and revisions of my own.

Rule 1. WATER IS OUR MAJOR HAZARD. DO *NOT* SWIM WITHOUT A COMPANION. DO NOT SWIM ALONE. I don't think this was a safety measure—I think Mr. Albert was the innovator of the singles weekends now used so unsuccessfully at Catskill Mountain resorts, resulting in many *enceinte yentas* and very few engagement rings. (When the shofar blows, so do the smooth-talking slickers from the garment district.)

IT IS EASY FOR SMALL CHILDREN TO FALL INTO THE LAKE, PARTICULARLY FROM THE BOATS AND THE DOCKS. A tip well worth remembering if you are being visited by a family who believe that a child's personality will become warped if the child's natural propensity for devastation and destruction is thwarted in any way.

IF THEY CANNOT SWIM, BE SURE THEY WEAR LIFE JACKETS WHEN OUT-OF-DOORS. A valid precaution, and we have just the life jacket for any little darling who sets fire to the couch or carves "Make Love Not War" in the dining-room table. Instead of kapok, it's filled with 23 pounds of ball bearings.

Rule 2. THE SECOND MAJOR HAZARD IS FIRE. WE ARE NOT PERMITTED TO BUILD A BONFIRE WITHOUT A PERMIT FROM THE DEPARTMENT OF LANDS AND FORESTS. STEP ON YOUR CIGARETTE OR YOUR CIGAR AND MAKE SURE THAT IT IS OUT. Not on the living-room rug, stupid!

Rule 3. This rule (about what to do if you get lost in the woods) has been covered elsewhere, but maybe we should add something: If you suddenly find that you are lost in the trackless forest with Elizabeth Taylor, don't panic. We'll find you. We'll give you a little time first. And then we'll look for you.

After Rule 3, Mr. Albert let everyone off the hook, insofar as the *hazardous* angle of a happy weekend in the vacationland of the north was concerned and he tried to make up for it with a few reassuring suggestions. In an aside he writes: COMPARED TO LIFE IN THE CITY, THERE ARE FEW PERILS AT LOST LAKE. WE GUARANTEE THAT YOU WILL NOT BE RUN OVER BY AN AUTOMOBILE (he makes no mention of being cut in half by some nut on water skis). AND YOU WILL NOT BE BOMBED (notice the wording *"be* bombed"—he was a good enough host not to write *"get* bombed"). AND YOU SHOULDN'T DEVELOP ULCERS OR HAVE A NERVOUS BREAKDOWN (unless you have to deal with the local household help).

Rule 4. BREAKFAST IS SERVED UNTIL NINE AND SELF-SERVE AFTER THAT. This is only a surmise, but from the size of the overstocked bar I would say there must have been a *lot* of self-serves. And a lot of slopped-over black coffee. Now here comes the part which gave me the thought that the Alberts must have lived like rulers of the realm at their cozy woodland fief: ANYONE PLANNING TO BE AWAY FOR THE DAY AT ANOTHER LAKE SHOULD ORDER LUNCHES THE NIGHT BEFORE. BELL IS RUNG FOR LUNCH AND DINNER, AND AT NINE AND THREE FOR THE CHAMPAGNE BREAK. *Champagne break!* Now all *we* get when we ring the bell at nine and three is an echo.

Rule 5. IN ONTARIO NO ADULT IS ALLOWED TO FISH WITHOUT A LICENSE. AS SOON AS POSSIBLE AFTER YOU ARRIVE, GIVE YOUR AGE, WEIGHT, ADDRESS, COLOR OF EYES, AND HEIGHT TO US, AND ONE OF OUR PILOTS WILL FLY IN AND PICK UP YOUR LICENSE. I wonder if the guests had to hold their own fishing poles, or did the Alberts have someone do it for you (during the champagne break at least)?

Rule 6. UNLESS YOU HAVE HAD EXPERIENCE REPAIRING OUTBOARDS, WE WOULD PREFER YOUR BRINGING A FAULTY MOTOR TO THE CHORE BOY. Where is that chore boy now—when we need him—to fix a faulty *everything!* Mr. Albert continues: THE CHORE BOY WILL SEE THAT EACH BOAT IS FUELED AND READY TO GO. We have the nine boats—inherited from the Alberts. They are *all* fueled and ready to go, but we have no people to go. I feel like a snuff concessionaire in an opium den. In a depressed area on the Riviera.

BE SURE YOUR ANCHOR IS SECURED TO THE ANCHOR ROPE BEFORE DROPPING THE ANCHOR. This is an excellent suggestion.

Rule 7. IF INSECTS ARE BAD, 6-12 SPRAY SHOULD BE USED. This doesn't keep insects away, but it lets them know you are aware that they are being naughty.

Which brings up a point. What the hell do insects eat when we're away for a few days? Are they cannibalistic, or do they just wait until we come back?

Rule 8. SOME OF THE CABINS HAVE KEROSENE-BURNING ALADDIN LAMPS. THEY FURNISH BETTER LIGHT BUT CAN BE A FIRE HAZARD. DO NOT USE THEM UNLESS YOU ARE IN THE ROOM AND BE SURE THEY ARE OUT WHEN YOU LEAVE THE ROOM OR GO TO SLEEP. These things are *really* called Aladdin lamps—it's stamped right on the metal. I rubbed one for hours one February evening, not really expecting a genie to show up, but after taking my nightly sleeping pill, I didn't discount this possibility. Of course, nothing happened except the note. The note was placed against the well-rubbed lamp and read: "You're just wasting your time. It's too cold up there"—signed: Raquel Welch, Vanessa Redgrave, Gina Lollobrigida, and Woody Allen. Woody Allen? Maybe I'd better forget the Seconals and switch to Ovaltine.

Rule 9. WE WOULD LIKE TO HAVE THE GENERATOR OFF BY 10:30 P.M. SINCE IT IS LOCATED NEAR THE WORK-PEOPLE WHO GET UP EARLY IN THE MORNING. The *work*people! The Alberts had a staff? Or maybe slaves? Way back here in the woods who would know? Except the slaves—and away back here in the woods, how could they be aware that somewhere out there behind those towering pines and balsams and hemlocks there was a world of unions, students for democratic riots, and other organizations that would release them from their slavery and get them on relief?

Rule 10. TRY TO REMEMBER TO BRING BACK YOUR FLASH-LIGHTS IN THE MORNING OR YOU MAY HAVE TO GO BACK TO YOUR CABIN IN THE DARK. Other people counted the silver after weekend guests left. Mr. Albert counted flashlights.

Rule 11. BAIT FOR FISHING: THE CHORE BOY WILL HELP YOU CATCH MINNOWS. Now *that* rubs me the wrong way.

Why can't the chore boy catch the minnows while I'm finishing my morning champagne? I don't mind roughing it, but a line must be drawn *somewhere!*

Rule 12. EVERYTHING YOU SEE IS FOR YOUR USE AND PLEASURE. I think Mr. Albert got this from the wall of an ancient Roman go-go joint. THE BAR IS ALWAYS OPEN.

Rule 13. OUR DRINKING WATER COMES FROM THE LAKE, SO KEEP IT CLEAN. Who cares—so long as the bar is always open?

These were the Alberts' rules to live by, at Lost Lake, and a copy of this list was posted on the wall of every cabin.

The Douglas family has only one rule for living at Lost Lake, and it doesn't have to be posted anywhere: KEEP CUTTING FIREWOOD!

12

THE cabin where I do my literary chores is a pleasant walk from the main lodge—during about four months out of the year. The rest of the time, it can be a polar expedition or slow drowning—depending on whether it is snowing or raining—but once I am there, inside, with my books and papers, and my ancient typewriter, it's very cozy and worth the trip.

My ancient typewriter, which at this writing, I am using to create funny stuff for *Laugh-In* and also a Jack Paar special, was given to me by my father, who had used it for years to

item which I thought *everybody* in New York would want to *buy* they had already *bought*. I was stuck with 400,000 CLERGY—ON CALL stickers for people who wanted to park their cars near the Radio City Music Hall. During Easter Week. (Have you ever seen the Rockettes dancing the Resurrection? Makes you feel as if you're really there.)

I was daunted but determined, so after the clergy sticker fiasco I took an option on 100 World War I surplus tanks, which I felt could be used for planters by militant little old ladies. This idea also flopped. The little old ladies didn't want surplus tanks—they wanted surplus machine guns, which were handier to use walking home from the bus stop after dark.

I'm still in the mail-order business, but only slightly. Whenever Fort Sumter needs more cannonballs I supply them. Thank God I was smart enough to anticipate *this* demand.

Back in the bush, I not only had time to think but time to remember. The quiet and peace which enveloped me like a huge balsam-scented womb invoked many pleasant memories, including my mother's balsam-scented womb, where if I hadn't been so perversely preadolescent, I should have stayed until I was ready for the world—and vice versa.

Every time Tanuki or one of our other wolves howled, I remembered Pat McCaughey, a wonderfully talented artist friend, who lived in California and who also had a pet wolf, whom he adored and who was adored, in turn, by the wolf, but dear Pat loved the sauce and spent most of his waking hours pleasantly mulled, while he painted and played with his pet. Then came the day of the big mistake. The big mistake was that Pat decided to quit drinking entirely, which apparently threw him off, creatively speaking. His work which was of the Pollock-De Kooning freaked-out school, started to make sense and immediately lowered his price, and his wolf, who loved him dearly, was so spooked by this cold sober apparition that he bit him. Pat immediately bought a case of Old Granddad and regained his artistic touch and the previous affection of his wolf, midway through the first bottle, and the last I heard he was once again the darling of Big Sur and the patron saint of wolfdom.

It was at about this time that I read about Robert David Lion Gardiner.

Robert David Lion Gardiner owns Gardiners Island, a large island situated between the eastern claws of Long

Island and reputed to be the burial plot for Captain Kidd's treasure. Mr. Gardiner, in an interview in one of the New York Sunday papers which I received at Lost Lake some two months after publication, confided to the interviewer that his island was overrun with deer and each fall it was necessary to kill about 300 of them to conserve the food supply of the main herd. When I read this, I immediately thought of the happening at Isle Royale National Park, a fascinating island, in the far reaches up upper Lake Superior. The moose on the island had gradually been depleting their food supply and strength by overbreeding. This tragic situation was remedied one extremely cold winter when a few wolves from Canada crossed the frozen lake and moved onto Isle Royale to stay. In a few short years the wolves, who can kill only the aged and infirm, in animals so large as a moose, had restored the balance of nature so well that some moose mothers were having twins, which is unusual. The wolf pack kept the moose herd within the limits in which it could sustain itself, and the wolves, who have practiced birth control long before it became unpopular with welfare recipients, kept their pack down to the level of the food supply ratio. Wolves, then, I thought might be the solution for Mr. Gardiner and his island's deer surplus, so I suggested this to him, posthaste.

Mr. Gardiner answered promptly. He said he just adored my suggestion, but doubted whether the wolves would get along with his tigers. The tigers, he explained confidentially, took care of the surplus weekend picnickers, who also overran his island. This is better than *ants*, and doesn't it conjure up a lovely picture? *Fade in* to a family picnicking in a secluded cove on Mr. Gardiner's island. Mother is laying out the messy goodies on a tablecloth spread on the ground. The children and Daddy are frolicking in the gentle surf. Suddenly Mother screams, "Harry! There are tigers all over the peanut butter and jelly sandwiches!" And Harry answers, "Stop yelling! Just brush 'em off! And open some beer!"

I have always had this "writing letters" thing like drunks have the long-distance telephoning thing—especially if it isn't their phone. I write to everybody whom I admire or disagree with. I know none of these people, but I'm always surprised at how many answers I get. And at the language.

Garbo answered me in a Lifebuoy-perfumed special delivery letter, which contained three perfectly blank pages. The fourth page was also blank, but at the top she had written "P.S."

Before we moved north to the Canadian bush country, I wrote to everyone and anyone who could give me some information about the rugged life. I wrote Anthony Greenbank, mountain climber and author of *The Book of Survival*, an excellent and exciting book, which should be on the library shelf of every 97-pound weakling. It won't help you gain weight, but it tells you exactly what to do if you are engulfed by an avalanche (don't panic), fall from an ocean liner in mid-ocean (don't panic), fall from a plane over Missouri (try to glide toward Kansas City), get lost in an underground cave (call Andy Warhol and make a movie), get caught in a forest fire (report it to Smokey), are buried alive (don't panic), and many other predicaments, which one can extract oneself from if one knows how—according to Anthony Greenbank. I wrote to him because I was fascinated by his helpful hints (listed in his book) on what to do if attacked by a wolf, which read in part: 1. Chop it on the *nose*. 2. Slam arm to back of jaws. 3. Go down with it, clutching back in crossed legs. 4. Squeeze like hell with legs and cause reflex backsquirm; then try jerking hand on neck.

I've tried this with my wolves, when they start to play too rough, and so far I've never got beyond No. 1: "Chop it on the *nose*." This usually makes them so mad I never get to No. 2. Sometimes I don't even complete No. 1. They interrupt my chop by seizing my chopper between their teeth and dragging me around like the female half of an Apache dance team. All they need is an orchestra playing "My Man."

I wrote Mr. Greenbank about this, and he replied that his method doesn't work with *pet* wolves, and I should really be a better sport about the whole thing and go out into the woods and find myself a nice *wild* wolf and at least give Mr. Greenbank's theory a chance. And also, if convenient, he would like some home movies (in color) of the encounter. I like Mr. Greenbank. And he'll be the third one to know if I chop a wild wolf on the nose. The first two will be the wild wolf and the coroner.

In the safe fastness of my little cabin office in the deep dark forest I have become very bold, or else I'm having wild spells of bush fever, because I write indiscriminately to kings and criminals, senators and sex fiends, queens and queers. So if you are a king or a criminal or a senator or a sex fiend or a queen or a queer, be patient, you'll hear from me. Or better still—why don't *you* write first for a change?

The vast amount of time I seemed suddenly to have inherited by moving away from the cluttered mainstream of twentieth-century living was an unexpected bonus and gave me the first chance in years to shovel my way through the tons of the very miscellaneous notes I had been making for centuries. These notes contained everything from brilliant ideas for plays or movies or television shows to esoteric, obscure, and sometimes absolutely unfathomable sentences pertaining to a permanently lost thought or observation. For instance, what did "Humpback drum majorette" have to do with anything? Is it code for something more sinister? Or is it merely an idea for a character I thought Tennessee Williams might use to arouse the dormant sex urge of my favorite Tennessee Williams' character—the three-foot dwarf with the four-foot penis? I'll *never know* and maybe it's just as well. A play with a humpback drum majorette might be hard to sell to theater parties.

13

ONE of our main problems at Lost Lake was Bobby. He had no one to play with. This, Reiko said, was sad. But then everything, to the Japanese, is sad. A rock is sad. A tree is sad. A sunset is sad. The wind and the rain and the moon are sad. I showed Reiko my bronzed baby shoes, and she thought they were sad. They *were* sad. I only had *one* and it was a size twelve. In our family, during the Depression, it was "Waste not, want not." You wore your baby shoes right through high school and sometimes right up to your junior year at Harvard, where you were considered quaint.

But getting back to the Japanese—something sad was the most fun they could have. A Japanese movie with the plague, an earthquake, a rape, a murder, an unwed mother, and an old Japanese patriarch disemboweling himself with a dull hari-kiri knife, sent them from the theater humming the blood.

"I don't think it's sad at all," I said, referring to Bobby, who at the moment was trying to make friends with a frog. He had also tried to make a pal out of a chipmunk, a snowshoe rabbit, and a moose. The moose was the least cooperative. So long as Bobby persisted in his Kiwanis-like clubability, the moose stayed away from his grazing area in back of my office. I was all for Bobby, but a bull moose, as tractable as it usually is, most of the year, during and after the fall mating season goes berserk and charges headlong at everything it considers a rival, including cars, trains, and large housewives transporting laundry on their heads, en route to their friendly neighborhood laundromat and hashish parlor.

"Look at him down there sitting on that rock, talking to a *frog!* Is that any life for a little boy?" Reiko said.

"Wait," I said. "Look at it from the frog's point of view— maybe talking to Bobby will make it a better frog."

"I think I go back Japan," Reiko said, which was her way of terminating any conversation not going her way.

The following weekend I hurt the frog's feelings by hauling in a couple of children for Bobby to play with. I almost said "neighborhood" children, but that would be stretching it. One, Jimmy Horse, the Indian trapper's little boy, whose name was Debbie, because Jimmy Horse's wife had once seen a Debbie Reynolds movie, in which Debbie Reynolds had played an Indian maiden. This was the same movie in which Sammy Davis, Jr., played Geronimo. And Burt Lancaster was the kindly old priest who converted the Indians to paganism. The other little boy, who, I convinced his parents, would have a jolly weekend in the country, like a fresh-air kid. I felt sort of silly, using this rationale, because the cabin they lived in hadn't been caulked for years, and the unpremeditated air conditioning kept blowing the tin plates off the table. But the Charbonneaus finally consented to allow their little boy, whom

they called Jo-Jo, to be led tearfully to the waiting Land
Rover and two days of fun with children, which was some-
thing he had never seen much of on the isolated shores of
Lac Lucie.

When we finally got the three children all together, Bobby
found that it was a lot easier communicating with a frog than
with Debbie, who spoke a combination of English, French,
and Ojibway, and Jo-Jo who didn't speak at all.

But both Debbie and Jo-Jo were fascinated by Bobby's
huge collection of broken toys, and pretty soon they were
all zooming bits of airplanes all over the room in a simulation
of the situation over a big-city airport. Debbie could manage
a bilingual dialogue with the control tower as he was about
to land: "Debbie Horse requesting permission to land. Roger.
Over and out." Jo-Jo just said, "Zoom. Zoom. Zoom," and
landed, which may have been the safest way. Bobby, with all
his worldly sophistication (comparatively), was more direct.
He just said, "These are my toys, and I'm gonna land first!"
The perfect host.

"Bobby," I said, "Debbie and Jo-Jo are your guests—you
must allow *them* to land first."

"Papa," he said, "you just don't understand. I live here—
I'm the boss."

"Boss," Debbie said.

"Zoom!" Jo-Jo said.

"You see," Bobby said, "Debbie and Jo-Jo know I'm the
boss."

"Jo-Jo just said, 'Zoom,' " I said.

"That's Indian language," Bobby said. "Jo-Jo's an Indian
boy."

"No, no," I said, "you're a little mixed up. Jo-Jo is French
Canadian; Debbie is an Indian boy. His father is Jimmy
Horse. He's the one who traps animals near here."

"I hope he doesn't trap my moose," Bobby said, then
zoomed away from the annoying jurisdiction of any further
parental interference with air travel.

At bedtime a crisis arose. Both Debbie and Jo-Jo became
homesick and started crying for their own little beds. They
didn't want to sleep with Bobby in one big bed. When I
started to explain that I couldn't take them home because it
was very dark outside, this was just the reason they wanted
to go home. It was very dark outside.

"Look," I said to Debbie, "you'll be just fine here—nice and warm and cozy—and after you get in bed, I'll tell you a bedtime story." Debbie stopped bawling long enough to give this some thought, while I said to Jo-Jo, "Jo-Jo likes it here. Jo-Jo wants to sleep in a big bed with Bobby and Debbie. Jo-Jo wants to hear Papa tell a bedtime story, don't you, Jo-Jo?" Jo-Jo grabbed a little toy airplane and zoomed past me right out the front door, running down the darkened path like a frightened deer. It took me three minutes to catch him and another twenty to drag him back to bedtime storyland. I thought of handcuffing him to the bed, but I am sure he would have told his mother and father, and I didn't want any French Canadians mad at me. They might have friends in the *plastique* bomb business in Montreal.

"Papa, it's getting late. What about the bedtime story?" Bobby said.

"I wanna hear about Goldilocks and the grizzlies," Debbie said.

"Grizzlies?" I said. "I never heard that version of Goldilocks."

"Indian-style bedtime story," Debbie said. "A lot more action. They eat her."

"I was thinking about 'The Boy Who Cried Wolf,' " I said.

"That's a good one," Bobby said.

"Do they *eat* him?" asked Debbie.

"They *sure do*," Bobby said.

"Zoom!" said Jo-Jo.

"Once upon a time," I started.

"*All* bedtime stories start off like that," Bobby informed his captive audience.

"I wanna glass of water," Debbie said, "from the well."

"Okay," I said, "but we don't have a well. We have a pump; the water comes out of the tap in the kitchen. Is that all right?"

Debbie thought about this, then: "Indian water comes out of a well."

"No," Bobby said, in a sage-flavored tone, "Indian water comes out of an Indian."

"Bobby," I said, "that's vulgar. It's clever, but it's vulgar."

"What's 'vulgar'?" Bobby said.

"Zoom!" Jo-Jo said.

"Now, come on," I said, " 'The Boy Who Cried Wolf.' Once upon a time—"

"Papa, you *told* us that already!" Bobby said.

"Anybody want ice cream?" Reiko said, interrupting with three mountainous dishes of chocolate, vanilla, and strawberry.

"What about 'The *Boy* Who Cried *Wolf*?'" I yelled.

"It doesn't matter," Reiko said. "They're *all* nice boys."

The "children" weekend was a success, but keeping our eyes on three healthy kids was a full-time problem. Debbie, the Indian boy, after boasting that he could lead a war party all the way to Sioux Lookout, through the dense forest, without getting lost, tried to prove it, and after a breathless, tense two hours we finally caught up with them, halfway between Lost and Loon lakes. They still had about 190 miles to go before they could sack and burn the little village of Sioux Lookout, but their spirit was strong and their matches were dry, and Reiko and I had a helluva time convincing Debbie and his two deputy warriors that they must honor the peace treaty made with the great white father, George III, although I really couldn't think of any good arguments *why*.

Jo-Jo had a thing for outboard motorboats, and the moment we turned to other essentials like the firewood supply or a few golden moments in cool meditation in the quiet of our one-and-only bathroom, Jo-Jo would be skimming the lake at the tiller of our fastest boat. He was impossible to catch, because our other boats were plodders, so our only choice was to pray that he didn't tear out the bottom of the speedster on one of the many shoals, and wait until the 25-horsepower motor had consumed its fuel. The first time this happened it took three hours and forty minutes. After that we made sure that only a teacup of gas was in the tank. This way the shipwreck factor was cut down to a bare minimum, but we still had to go out and tow his becalmed craft back to our safe harbor. This became a bore after the first few times, and toward the end we left him out there in the middle of the lake to think things over.

Jo-Jo must have thought things over quite thoroughly because he learned where we kept the marine gas and filled his tank to the brim before he took off again.

I asked Debbie, the Indian boy, if he would like to paddle

a canoe and he said, "What's a canoe?" I knew then it would be useless to ask him if he wanted to try a little archery.

After the novelty, for Debbie and Jo-Jo, had become a commonplace, and Bobby became no longer curious about his weekend playmates, all three of them went off on their own, and late Sunday afternoon I discouragedly watched all three of them. Each alone in a separate section of our little island, sitting at the edge of the lake, talking earnestly to three different frogs.

When I took Debbie and Jo-Jo back to their homes, Mr. and Mrs. Jimmy Horse said to Debbie, "Did you have a good time?"

Debbie said, "Yeah. Boy, they got a lotta frogs up there."

Jo-Jo's answer to his parents was more succinct and a lot more graphic. When Mr. and Mrs. Charbonneau asked Jo-Jo what he had been doing all weekend, he just said, "Zoom!"

_14_

I LOVE Canada, or maybe I should say I love the idea of Canada—a vast territory of 3,851,809 square miles and with a tiny population of only 20,000,000 people, most of them strung out along its southern borders, where it is hoped they will stay.

This, I'm sure, is not the will of the Canadian government. But this is the way _I'd_ like it, after seeing what the uncontrolled overpopulation of California has done to that once-magnificent state. Fred Allen said, "California is all right if you're an orange." This is no longer true—if you're an orange, you'd shrivel and die for lack of oxygen. California's fabled former climate was its undoing. If the ones who discovered it had kept their big mouths shut instead of hiring press agents by the thousands to shout about it, maybe there would be some of it left untouched by shopping centers, liquor stores, bowling alleys, and Muscle Beach movies. But enough of this mewling over the glorious West that Harry Cohn knew and loved.

The meteorological climate of Canada will never change it to anything but what it is, unless God and some Japanese steel company make a deal to put an astrodome over the whole thing.

A U.S. Senator, from Rhode Island, I believe, wanted to do this in the United States. He felt that if we could afford some of the other things we had, why not have the first indoor country. The idea died in committee when it was discovered how much the air conditioner would cost. The Senator, in a moment of lucidity, conceded we must draw the line somewhere and proposed the abandonment of the astrodome project, voicing the opinion that the money would be much better spent fighting pollution of Beverly Hills swimming pools (suntan oil is making them undrinkable). The committee is appointing a committee to investigate this.

A few chauvinists will undoubtedly take umbrage because at the moment I prefer to live in Canada. I should not dignify their attitude, but what would be the fun if I didn't? So far as I am concerned, Canada is just the northern part of the United States, or to put it in another bristle-making way, the United States is just the southern part of Canada. There— now I have both countries mad at me.

Living in Canada reminds me of the time I was playing at a variety theater in Scotland in the long ago. I was doing a comedy act, but from the reaction of the Scots this was a doubtful and paranoiac assumption on my part. I found later in the pubs and also in the homes of these people why there was deadly silence every time I was at, I thought, my comedic best, in the theater. It was because I was an American, which, in Scotland, was the same as being English, which was the same thing as being an apprentice leper. But this attitude was only found in large gatherings. Individually, the Scotsman had no such antipathy toward an American. This is true also of the Canadian. Collectively, I feel he has little use for the American—collectively. But one at a time, he goes out of his way to be helpful and kind.

Farley Mowat, the bearded Canadian writer who wrote, among many other things, a lovely, humorous, and compassionate book about wolves and his experiences with them in the far north district of Keewatin, which is a little farther north than anyone usually cares to go, is a splendid example of a Canadian who thrives on taking Americans apart. Not to see what makes them tick. Just to make them holler. Mr. Mowat and I have been pen pals for quite some time, and when he publicly dips his scalpel in contaminated owl's blood and writes an unholy diatribe about us damn Yankees, I don't mind, because he is someone who also cares deeply about what happens to the wild creatures still left on this earth, and he also cares about what happens to *us* way back in the bush. His thoughtful advice has helped us muddle through.

But back to the tall timber and its many surprises—like the blackfly season. The blackfly season starts on May 15 and lasts three weeks until June 7. Blackflies are as punctual as those strange California swallows that, according to the song and a few strange California monks, always arrive at the San Juan Capistrano Mission on exactly the same day each year. A strange story—unless you're a Californian. Californians still believe in the Easter bunny and Santa, but inversely, they think God is a rerun.

The blackfly season doesn't sound like much of a problem unless you've lived through one of these three-week periods. On May 15 suddenly billions of these insidious little devils come into being.

During this period of the blackfly invasion you cannot go outside the house unless you wear rubber bands around the ankles of your slacks and your shirt and your neck and also you must wear a hat with a mosquito netting veil. Everybody goes around looking like a nervous witness at a Mafia investigation. Or the widow at a cheap funeral. Some doubters, of course, don't believe in the blackfly's proliferation or potency. We had a girl visitor during those three weeks last spring who dared to get off the plane in a mini-skirt. Of course, ever since, whenever she's asked the delicate question of how she lost her virginity, *no one* believes her story. Poor thing. She still giggles a lot and walks like Henry Fonda.

One cool, sun-splashed morning we heard the sound of a plane overhead. This was not unusual, but I must confess that every time we hear a plane, we all rush outside to see if it is going to land and visit. And this time was no exception. We rushed outside. The plane, which seemed to be crisscrossing the surrounding territory, was like none we had ever seen before. The body and wings were a mass of what looked like wireless antenna, while about 200 feet below it dangled a bomb on a long rope.

"What the hell are *they* up to?" I said.

"Looks like a bomb," Reiko said.

"Looks like a bomb on a string," Bobby said.

The plane circled in ever-narrowing circles and passed low over our little island about five times before it reeled in the bomb and landed on the lake and floated up to the plane dock. I had Reiko wait in the house with her rifle at the ready, which at the moment I thought was necessary, while I sauntered (like a stalking Iroquois) down to the dock, with my .38 police special tucked in my back pocket.

When the plane's pontoons nudged the dock, a handsome, tanned young giant jumped out and made her fast. Then Wally Cox felt his way down the side of the two-engine survey plane. By this time I knew what kind of plane it was and its purpose. It was a mineral survey plane, and the dangled bomb was a magnetometer, an instrument which picks up magnetic variations that can point the way to deposits of nickel, copper, zinc, lead, and other valuable metals.

Tanned and Handsome got back into the plane, and the Wally Cox impersonator extended a damp palm and explained that they were surveying the area for the presence of metals.

"Then you've come about the uranium deposit," I said. The little man blanched, and his palms got damper.

"You *know* about the uranium?" he said.

"Yeah," I said. "For a couple of years at least."

"Why didn't you say something?"

Reiko came out the front door and called, "Jack-san, how about the rifle?"

"It's okay," I said. "You can put it away."

"You don't have to guard uranium like that," said Professor Swayne, the name on his card.

"We don't worry about that," I said. "We're just careful when we have unexpected visitors."

"Oh," said Professor Swayne, trying to force a smile on a face that wasn't used to that kind of carryings-on. "Where is your uranium deposit?"

"I don't know whether I should tell you," I said.

"We'll find it anyway," the professor said. "Besides, you don't own it, y'know."

"Oh, yes, we do, Professor. Mrs. Albert gave it to us."

"Who's Mrs. Albert?"

"She is the former owner. When she left for the last time she said, 'Jack, it's yours and good luck.'"

"But," the professor said, "it wasn't hers to give. All minerals under the land and all the timber above the land in a wilderness reserve belong to the queen. Queen Elizabeth!"

"Look," I said, "Professor, before you give yourself palpitations, why don't you sit right down and write to her and ask her if she wants it? If she does, I'll send it to her."

"The queen? . . . I—I, I don't even know her."

"So what?" I said. "She'll be tickled pink to hear from somebody from Canada—it's probably been a long time."

"Oh," the professor said, suddenly becoming aware that I was having my little joke.

"Come on," I said. "I'll show you the uranium deposit." I led him into the house and behind the door where we had a large black rock, which we used for a doorstop. I kicked it. "There it is," I said. "Try your handy-dandy Geiger counter on that."

The professor whipped out something that looked like a stopwatch with generator attached. He held it next to the rock and flipped a switch. Immediately the thing came alive with a machine-gun rattle of click-click-clicks. That rock was loaded.

"Where," the professor stuttered, "did this rock come from?"

"Elliot Lake," I said. Elliot Lake is the site of one of the largest uranium strikes in recent years. "Mrs. Albert got it from a friend of hers who's got a whole lot of them up there at Elliot Lake."

"Elliot Lake," Professor Swayne said. "It's always Elliot Lake! It's never anywhere *I* look! I've combed this goddamn bush country from here to the Yukon for twelve years now, and do you know what I've found?"

"What?" I said, with perfect timing.

"Nothing!" The professor sobbed. "Nothing! Absolutely nothing!"

"Why don't you go someplace else?" Bobby said.

The professor tried to pull himself together. "Like where? Where can I go?"

"Connecticut," Bobby said. "They got a lot of rocks there. All colors."

Wally Cox suddenly became General Rommel. "Whose child is this?"

"His name is Bobby," Reiko said, sticking with the Japanese style of never giving a direct answer to anything.

"Where did this child come from?" General Rommel demanded.

"He's a rental," I said. "You see—I went into the Hertz agency one day and they were all out of Chevy coupes—"

General Rommel collapsed into a pool of *Weltschmerz* and came out Wally Cox. A sad, sad Wally Cox. I felt sorry for him. I envisioned the years of grueling geological study and the decade of searching the vast north country only to discover three kooks living back in the woods with a uranium-filled doorstop. It was enough to make a strong man cry, but Professor Swayne controlled himself until he got back to the survey plane and Handsome Harry. Then he broke down completely and Handsome Harry picked him up like a baby and hoisted him into the plane. The last we saw of Professor Swayne he was sobbing himself to sleep in the back of the luggage compartment, sucking on his blanket and hugging his Teddy bear.

15

OF the thirteen islands in Lost Lake, we own twelve. The thirteenth island is owned by a very stubborn psychiatrist, who will not sell. The other 4,000 square miles of the North Chinook Bay Wilderness Reserve, in which Lost Lake is located, is the property of the queen, who is very stubborn also. We wanted to buy two acres on the mainland for a vegetable garden, but she wouldn't part with one lousy square inch. So in memory of Patrick Henry, I sneak out every night and plant a few cucumbers and string beans. I would like to plant corn, but it grows too tall and might be spotted from the air by a U-2 plane.

The thirteenth island, which I irrationally coveted, was owned by Dr. Herbert Shrady, who was reputed by Charlie Burke to be a psychiatrist, although Charlie, for once, didn't seem too sure of his facts, and there was little about Dr. Shrady's snug log cabin, with its painted hex signs, snuggled cozily in the shelter of a delightful grove of pines and birches, to indicate his chosen branch of medical dedication (except Wednesdays and weekends). Although the two huge Indian totem poles, which were placed on each side of the stone walk up from his landing, were carved with Indian gods whose faces looked less like gods and more like patients.

Dr. Shrady, who lived next to Ed and Pegeen Fitzgerald, in Kent, Connecticut, only visited his island cabin for two weeks each August, which he said was long enough, and I was inclined to agree.

Dr. Shrady, to give him the best of it, must be classified as an eccentric. He referred to himself as a nut. "I'm the nut who gets paid for telling other nuts that they're nuts." Wishing to establish a little common ground between us, and also maybe in some sort of inverse self-defense, I told him that I had read all the Horney books.

"Good for you," he said. "How did you like *Candy?*"

This shook me up a bit, and I said, "I was referring to *Dr.* Horney."

"Of course," he said, "nice chap."

"I meant Dr. *Karen* Horney," I said. "I was always under the impression that she was a woman."

"Oh?" Dr. Shrady said. "You *do* have a problem, don't you?"

Dr. Shrady, who owned a 10-foot rowboat with a 50-horse-power, supercharged outboard motor, which all but dragged the tiny craft under, fancied himself as a navigator on the same immortal level as Columbus, Magellan, and Ulysses. This legend was shattered the first time he volunteered to pilot me around Lost Lake to acquaint me with the various shoals, which might prove dangerous to navigation.

"Quite a few dangerous shoals in this lake," he said, as he gunned the little boat full speed into a colony of jagged rocks. "There's one now."

The boat was made of tough fiber glass, and although badly bulged, it did not split wide-open like any other less sensitive craft might have done. The Gargantuan outboard motor had been wrenched off and was presumably at the bottom of the lake, but even though the motor had torn off most of the stern, we were in no immediate peril, unless the beavers got really eager and raised the water level of the lake another inch and a half. After a few embarrassing moments (to me) while we just sat there looking at the rocky prongs that held us and the little boat like we had been set there by that great master jeweler in the sky, I felt I should say *something* to this gung ho navigator.

"Got plenty of insurance?" I said, thus becoming, with four short words, the boor's boor. Why couldn't I have said something like "Good strong boat" or "Touché" or "Lot of new rocks around here this year"?

The doctor wasn't at all disturbed by my apparent compassion deficiency.

"Don't worry," he said. "I am insured for *everything.*"

"Good," I said.

"The only trouble is," he said, "every time I mention anything that resembles a claim, I find out that the only thing I am really covered for is vandalism by Martians."

"Maybe we could make up some kind of story," I said. "Like we were driven up on the rocks by a typhoon."

"It wouldn't do any good—my insurance company doesn't pay off even on the truth."

"Why don't you write to the Connecticut Insurance Department—up in Hartford? They're supposed to take care of any irregularities."

"Ha!" the doctor snorted. "I *did* write to them—and you know what happened?"

"What?" I said.

"Nothing—they're all *Martians*."

I felt from my own experience with this bureaucratic body that the doctor could be right, and anyone who dared to ask a civil question about the decisions of a Hartford-based insurance company immediately became reclassified as a poor risk.

"Doctor," I said, giving some thought to our rocky predicament, "has this ever happened to you before?"

"Of course," he said. "And I know exactly what to do. Fly the flag upside down—that's a distress signal. Anybody sailing by will see it and stop to help us."

"*Who's* gonna sail by?" I said.

"Jack," he said. "I'm only a doctor—not a soothsayer."

"Doctor," I said, "there's nobody else on this lake but us—and maybe nobody else within fifty miles. And we don't have a flag to fly upside down or a flagpole to fly it upside down on."

"Relax, Killjoy, I'm ready for that, too." He dived into a large wooden box and came up with what looked like a Roman candle. "It's a distress rocket," he said, touching a match to its fuse, and in no time at all the thing exploded with a loud whoosh and knocked off the rest of the back of the boat.

"Oops," he said. "That's what Dr. Freud used to say a lot when he was first starting." Dr. Shrady had put a match to the second rocket and was waving it toward me for emphasis.

"I'm grateful for that little insight," I said, hitting the bottom of the boat as the second rocket skipped along the tip of the water for a few hundred feet before it exploded with a fizzle and sank.

"Aren't you supposed to shoot those things up in the air?"
I asked.

"For the best result, yes," he said.

The third rocket got off to a good start, more or less in
the direction of the heavens, and detonated with a loud report
which echoed back and forth among the rocky coves of the
lake. We waited for a good half hour, but no one showed up
to see what all the rocketry was about. Dr. Shrady fired his
fourth, and last, rocket. The explosion from this one was
much louder than the others.

"That's the large family-size distress signal," the doctor
said. "That ought to make 'em come running." But it didn't.
We sat there for another hour; then we started to shout. Our
voices echoed back and forth in the large cove we were
rock-wrecked in, but evidently nobody heard them except us.
In another hour neither one of us could talk above a whisper.
We gave up. We had to. With a whisper you don't get much
of an echo.

The sun was about twenty minutes from disappearing behind the dark pines of the western shores when we heard the
low hum of an outboard motor, and in a few minutes Jake
came around the point. He was heading for our garbage dump
farther up the lake. We waved at him. He waved back. Then
we waved frantically, and he waved back and continued on
his way to the garbage dump.

"I'll kill the sonofabitch," I said.

"I'll help you," the doctor said. "But first we have to lure
him close enough to grab him."

On his way back from the garbage dump Jake steered his
boat over to ours.

"Any luck?" he said.

"Any luck?" I screamed from my bleeding throat. "Can't
you see we're stuck on the rocks? And why the hell didn't
you come when you saw our rockets?"

"I thought it was some Yank celebrating the Fourth of
July."

"This is August," I said.

"Gee whiz," he said. "I'm supposed to be on my *vacation!*"

On the way back to drop Dr. Shrady at his island cabin,
he started talking to me out of the side of his mouth, like
Humphrey Bogart in stir.

"I'd like to get this guy on the couch," he said. "I'd like to find out what's going on inside his head."

"Why don't you get him on an operating table and just saw off the top of his skull?" I said out of the other side of *my* mouth.

"I *been* analyzed," Jake said, out of both sides of his mouth. This sort of put a damper on any further stir talk.

The next day we almost got our wish in regard to the inside of Jake's head. He had condescended to cut a little firewood in case it should get chilly the next winter, and somehow he slipped, and the tree he was cutting, unfortunately a smallish one, crashed down and creased his skull. We knew nothing of this until he came up to the lodge about dusk with his head swathed in grimy bandages.

"Look, Papa," Bobby said, "a guru!"

"What happened?" Reiko said.

"Have you got any whiskey?" Jake said, trying to faint.

"Only for emergencies or friends," Reiko answered. "That's what Jack-san said."

After Jake had sorted out which category he was in, he said, "A tree fell on me."

We had no way of verifying this, and knowing his predilection for the sauce that refreshes, I felt that whole thing might be a put-on, so I said, "Yeah, we have whiskey, but first tell us about this, and where's the firewood?"

"It's still in the tree that fell on me. It's layin' out there in the bush with blood all over it. It's covered with blood—all *over* it. It's *real bloody*," he said.

"Will it still burn?" I said.

He didn't answer, so I gave him a slug of whiskey, and this changed his whole attitude toward the world in general and firewood in particular. He promised, eyeing the bottle, that he would be out there in the bush first thing in the morning and cut ten cords before noon. I felt that, in view of past performances, we'd be lucky to see a half a cord before nightfall, but I gave him another slug, took him to the front door, and steered him in the direction of his cabin, hoping that with his fractured skull and two shots of booze, he would misstep on the little footbridge which connected us with the mainland and disappear into the darkening waters of the lake. But with all his well-publicized afflictions, he was as surefooted as a welfare recipient bounding up to the payoff window of his friendly neighborhood unemployment office just before a holiday weekend. He made it all the way to his cabin, and just before he opened his door, he took off his bandages and tossed them into a trash pail. I liked that, because now I knew he couldn't use that sly bit again, and I licked what chops I had left, in anticipation of what form his next wily device would take in order to get himself a sympathetic mug of moon juice. Too bad he couldn't plead snakebite because we were just a little too far north for anything more venomous than some lovely little green ones plus a few common garter snakes.

In the two weeks that Dr. Shrady and his wife, Mildred, stayed at their Lost Lake cabin we saw them almost every day, although when it came to a suggested cruise, I left the driving to me. Mildred confided that in the twenty or so years they had been coming to Lost Lake, the good doctor had managed to sink one or two boats every year, and she said he seemed quite disappointed that his average was so low.

The doctor's idea of fun, when he wasn't busily sinking fleets, was his hidden tape recorder, with the recorded sound of Godzilla, or some other fearful prehistoric monster, who appears frequently in Japanese-made science-fiction-sex movies, on tape. This frightening creature, who is usually brought back to life (in the movie) because of some man-made atomic malfunction, appearing over the horizon, emitting horrific screams and exhaling polluted fire, ripping Tokyo into tiny bits of flaming rubble, then resisting all attempts to kill it with barrages of nuclear war-headed rockets, finds its baby, which some evil promoter has had on exhibition at the Tokyo Marineland, and together the flame-shooting prehistoric monster and her son go peacefully back to the Black Lagoon or some other undersea senior citizen village.

The sound of this monster at its most terrifying was what the doctor had on tape—the recorder being hooked up to an *extremely loud* speaker hidden back in the trees near his cabin. When the doctor was lucky enough to be entertaining people who had never been to the Lost Lake retreat before, he would activate Mother Godzilla's enraged shrieking by pressing a concealed button behind the bar as he was apparently engaged in pouring everyone another round.

We were there one night when the Shradys were hosting some tenderfoots, who had just flown up from Darien and Westport. Doc waited until there was a decided lull in the gay conversation of the first night of a weekend in the woods. From his control center behind the bar he pressed the magic button and immediately there was the sound of a *tyrannosaurus* in a blind fury coming up the garden path.

The couple from Westport froze. "What was that?????" The couple from Darien kept drinking.

"What was what?" the doctor said, pressing the button again.

"That!!!!!" The Westport couple screamed and clawed at him for deliverance. The couple from Darien sweetened up their drinks and forged ahead.

"Oh, that," the doctor said. "It's nothing—we hear it every once in a while. It's supposed to be some creature—like the Loch Ness monster. It lives here in Lost Lake. According to what the Indians say."

"Indians!" the Westport wife whimpered, unconsciously putting her hand to her blue rinse hair job to see if it was still there.

"For crissakes! Indians!" the Westport husband said. "They drink a lot—you gonna believe *them?*"

"It's just a legend," the doctor said. "Indians have many legends. That's all they have left—legends." He pressed the button again.

"That's no legend," the Westport wife said. "And it's getting closer! Baldwin, you've got to *protect* me!"

"Why *me?*" the Westport husband said.

"We had a Loch Ness monster in our family once," the Darien husband said, "but she died."

"Who was that, dear?" the Darien wife said.

"Your mother," the Darien husband said.

"Oh, yes," the Darien wife said, "lovely service as I remember it. It was on a Saturday morning. I remember it was a Saturday because we didn't tee off until almost ten thirty."

"They took her to the cemetery in a golf cart," Doc whispered to me as he pressed the button again. This time, with full volume on, the windows of the cabin chattered and a shot glass fell off the bar. The Westport couple started packing, and the Darien couple turned on the television set to catch the last twenty-seven reels of *The Glenn Miller Story.* Mildred went to the kitchen to shovel up another pail of clam dip, while Doc explained to the Westport couple that even if they packed, it would be dangerous to try and leave the island while the "thing" was outside.

"Can'tcha do something!" the Westport husband said. "You're a *psychiatrist!*"

"There's nothing to be alarmed about," Doc patiently explained. "For all we know, the whole thing might just be a myth. A figment of someone's imagination."

"Oh, yeah," the Westport wife said, "then what the hell is that horrible screaming noise?"

"Mice," Doc said. "You see, up here in the north country the air is so pure and clear everything sounds louder. There's no smog or other pollution to muffle the sound—care for another drink?"

"I never heard mice like that in Westport sound like that," the Westport husband said, as he accepted a double scotch on the rocks. "They just squeak."

"The mice in Westport," Dr. Shrady said, in silky-smooth reassuring couchside tones, "are conditioned to 'just squeak' —because of a repressive ordinance passed way back in 1720 by the early settlers. They had had enough of loud mice back in the Massachusetts Colony because Cotton Mather didn't know what to do about them. In Massachusetts they knew how to hang witches, but they never figured out how to hang a mouse."

"How about by the tail?" suggested the Darien husband.

"Tail?" the Darien wife said, semibrightly—apparently aroused from the depths of some sweet scotch-mist reverie.

"Yes," said Dr. Shrady, "I said, in Massachusetts they never figured out how to—"

"Oh, goodie," the Darien wife said, "Dr. Shrady is gonna tell us about one of his nice juicy cases."

"No, I'm not!" Dr. Shrady said.

"I wish we'da gone to Hawaii like we planned instead of coming up here," the Darien wife pouted.

"You wouldn't like Hawaii," the doctor said. "It's a musical comedy elephant graveyard."

"What the hell does that mean?" the Westport wife said.

"It's the only state in the Union which carries the death penalty for playing the ukulele," said the doctor, who seemingly was always ready to launch into a nightclub routine on any subject.

"What?"

"Every hotel on Waikiki Beach employs a 'Hate' pro."

"How about the palm trees?" the Darien husband said.

"Plastic."

"What about the hula-hula dancers?" the Westport husband asked. "They sure wiggle their asses."

"Foam rubber," Doc said.

"What the hell *is* real in Hawaii?"

"The prices."

"Gee," the Darien wife said, "it doesn't sound romantic at all."

"Oh, but it is," Doc said. "But not like it used to be. Do you know that in the old days the natives had to force the missionaries to wear clothes."

"I never read *that* in the *National Geographic*," the Westport wife said.

"I know," Doc said. "They *never* betray a confidence."

Just as the party was getting back to normal a loud, shrill, eerie tremolo moan rose and fell somewhere outside.

"Jesus, what was that!" Doc said. "I didn't even push the button."

"It's an owl," said Mildred, who had just come in with a fresh pail of clam dip. "A prehistoric owl—eighty feet tall with five-foot talons. It's gonna grab up this whole cabin and drop it in the middle of Hudson Bay just for laughs."

"But why?" the Westport wife said, not quite sure of what Mildred meant.

"Because prehistoric owls have a perverted sense of humor. Dropping cabins full of innocent tourists into Hudson Bay is their idea of fun," Mildred said.

"Oh, I see," the Westport wife said. "It's a joke, huh?" Mildred just sighed.

Bobby was asleep on the floor, as usual next to a polar bear rug (it seemed you had to have a polar bear rug plus a rack of moose horns if you expected to run a proper "in" camp in the north country), and Reiko was sitting with a fixed smile, not knowing what to make of all the weirdo conversation she had heard. Poor little thing, she had spent so many of these frustrating evenings. After a while she would just give up and nod politely and smile politely and wish she was home in bed watching the late movie. I've often wished the same thing, but I was enjoying myself this night because I knew that sooner or later Dr. Shrady would do something historical and I wanted to be around when he did. This was his last night at Lost Lake, so he really didn't have much time, but I thought he might still come through.

Just when I was about to give up and go home to bed (to watch the last reel of *The Glenn Miller Story*), two men walked in the door.

"Oh, hi there," Doc said. "What are you drinking?"

"Huh," the tall red-haired one said.

"I'll have a Coke if you got it," said the short dark man.

"Yeah, me too," said Big Red. "Oh, we're—we just escaped from Washburn—you know the, er, honor farm."

"That's quite a walk," I said.

"Yeah," said Big Red. "That's why we had to steal a car."

"Well, how'd you get *here?*" the Westport wife said, from behind her husband, who was behind a dead rubber plant. "This is an island."

"We had to steal a boat, too," the small dark one said. "Oh—my name is Pierre, and this is Big Red."

Everyone shook hands, and I thought, well, so far it wasn't starting out like *The Desperate Hours,* but how it would end was, at that time, a moot question. The two escapees looked like escapees. They both had a couple of days' growth of beard, and they were dirty and tattered and forlorn.

"Are you hungry?" Mildred asked, offering the pail of clam dip.

"No," they both said, rather too quickly.

"What's the next move?" I said, not too anxious to know.

"We're headin' for Georgian Bay. We figure we can steal a boat there and maybe make it across to the States."

"That's ridiculous," Doc said. "There are no boats over along the Georgian Bay shore, because there are no people there—except maybe a few Indians."

"Don't they have boats?" said Big Red.

"Sure, but it might take you a long time to find one."

"Gee whiz," said Little Pierre, "I thought this was gonna be easy."

"That's a helluva long trip," I said. "To get to the States you have to cross Georgian Bay and then Lake Huron."

"You'd have to steal the *Queen Mary*," Doc said. "And the *Queen Mary* is in Long Beach, California."

"What's it doin' there?" Big Red wanted to know.

"John Wayne uses it to get to Catalina."

"I like John Wayne," Little Pierre said, his bright black eyes filling with love.

"I like Mia Farrow," Big Red said. His nostrils widened and his ears flattened when he said this.

"Sure," Little Pierre said, "but you been at Washburn a lot longer than I have."

"You'd better go back to the honor farm," I said. "They're gonna grab you no matter what. There's only one road, and the police are sure to be watching that, and you just can't cross all that water."

"Maybe we could spend the winter *here*," Little Pierre said. *This is what I need,* I thought, *two escaped convicts for neighbors. I'm sure they'd always be dropping in to borrow something. Even if we weren't home.*

"That's no good," Reiko said. "You'd have to have a fire, and Charlie Burke might fly by and see the smoke and get suspicious."

"I don't even know Charlie Burke and I don't care if he gets suspicious," Big Red said. "We're *stayin'!*"

"We're leaving tomorrow morning," Doc said. "My two weeks' vacation is up, and it's back to the old grind," he added, in the most falsely jolly tone I have ever heard.

"You *can't* leave," Big Red said.

"Why not?"

"Because you'll *tell.*"

"Tell *what?*"

"Tell you *seen* us."

"Look," Doc said, "I live in Kent, Connecticut, and I'm sure that even if I tell everybody in town, not one of them will give a good goddamn. Even if you escaped from the Kent jail, they wouldn't give a good goddamn."

"Gee," Little Pierre said. "That kinda takes all the fun out of it."

"Maybe so," Big Red said, "but this group ain't leavin' until *we* find a way to get clean away from here."

"Okay," Doc said, "I'm having a drink—anybody else want one?"

Everybody wanted one this time, and as the good doctor,

always the perfect host, busied himself behind the bar, the tight silence of the little cabin was suddenly blasted by the horrifying scream of a prehistoric monster. Little Pierre sprang into the hairy arms of Big Red who, in turn, leaped to the mantelpiece and crouched there, cradling Little Pierre —a baboon Madonna and Child.

"She's nervous tonight," the doctor said. "Here are your drinks, gentlemen." Big Red dropped Little Pierre and belted down both their whiskeys. Little Pierre lay on the floor, in fetal position, as *Tyrannosaurus rex* roared once more.

"Fill 'em up again," Big Red said to the doctor.

"Of course," Dr. Shrady said.

"I never heard nothin' like that in my life before. What— what is it?" Big Red said.

The sound came again. Louder. And closer.

"That," the doctor said, "is the Lost Lake monster. Or so they say. We've been hearing about him for years. Supposed to be some sort of gigantic lizard. Only with teeth. Weighs about eighty tons. Teeth six inches long. Eats meat."

Little Pierre was crossing himself—which was hard to do in a fetal position.

Doc pressed the button once more, and suddenly we were back to our original group. It was as though Big Red and Little Pierre had never been there at all.

"Somebody left," the Darien wife said.

"Pleasant chaps," the Darien husband said. "Tense though. Very tense."

"Everybody's crazy," Reiko said.

"Thank God," Dr. Shrady said.

16

I HAVE an agent, who has been misguiding my theatrical career for the past twenty years. Whatever he has suggested has been disastrous, but I love him like a favorite wart. His name is Irving Laveeeene, which is the most far-out spelling of Levine I have ever come across. Irving is only about four feet eleven, but he seems shorter because of his elevator shoes. He is tremendously successful and is rarely seen except in the company of the peers of the realm of show business, but for some reason, he has never lost the common touch, which is well represented by me. He is an extremely unique human being, and if he had lived during the Wars of the Roses, he would have been representing both sides—like an aphid.

Irving, I had heard from Abel Green, the padre of *Variety*, was on the verge of a nervous breakdown from too many crises brought on mainly by performers who had suddenly become hot—everywhere except in intelligence. Simple hog callers, overnight, through the miracle of electronics, had become song screamers and had screamed themselves, with the aid of *one* hit record, into the multimillionaire class and were demanding equal time with Richard Nixon, Pope Paul, and Pamela Tiffin.

All this had worn Irving down into a quivering mass of indecisive and unnerved Jello. Irving had to get away, Abel told me. When I suggested the Lost Lake and North Chinook Bay Wilderness Reserve, Abel had his doubts. And so did I, but the next afternoon Charlie Burke was bruising his Cessna's rubber bumpers against our dock, and Irving climbed shakily down from the little craft's interior.

"Got a telephone?" were Irving's first words.

"Sure," I said, "but you won't be able to use it until late this afternoon."

"I gotta use it *now*," Irving said. "I gotta call Paul and Joanne. I got a great movie for them to do. Remember 'Little Miss Muffet'?"

"Intimately," I said.

"Well, Mike Nichols got this great idea—you take 'Little Miss Muffet' and make it into an allegory."

"Who's Paul and Joanne?" Reiko said.

"What's an allegory?" I said.

"What's a Muffet?" Bobby said.

"Paul *Newman* and Joanne *Woodward*," Charlie Burke said.

"What's your name, son?" Irving said.

"Charlie Burke," Charlie said.

"You're *smart*," Irving said. "Rustic—but smart."

"Okay," Charlie said, "here's your bag. I gotta fly over to Kerry and pick up a hunter who got himself shot by another hunter."

Leaving us with this bit of good news, Charlie taxied out into the lake and was gone.

"Where's the phone?" Irving said. "Come on. This idea is hot. I don't want to blow it."

"Little Miss Muffet?" Reiko said.

"Yeah," Irving said, "in this allegorical treatment that Jackie Susann is going to give it, Little Miss Muffet is a junkie."

"Oh, I know that one," Bobby said. " 'Little Miss Muffet sat on a tuffet, eating her curds and whey.' "

"That's it," Irving said, "but she doesn't eat curds and whey—she smokes pot."

"That *is* cute," I said.

"You think so?" Irving said, plunging on without waiting for my answer. "If we can get Mike Nichols to direct this picture—"

"Wait a minute," I said. "You want *Mike Nichols* to direct *Paul Newman?*"

"Why not?" Irving said. "Florabel Muir said that Mike Nichols is the greatest thing since Jesus!"

"Maybe he should direct a Biblical picture then," I said. "If you could get Shelley Winters to play the Virgin Mary."

"Are you *sick!*" Irving said. "Shelley Winters—the Virgin Mary? What's the matter with Bette Davis?"

"Yeah," I said, "or Rod Steiger."

"No," Irving said, his eyes narrowing. "Bette Davis would be all wrong—somehow I just can't picture her in the manger, waving that goddam cigarette around."

"Paul Newman is a nice man," Reiko said. "He sat all the way through Jack-san's play in Westport."

"Maybe he's a little crazy," I said, following Irving up the path from the airplane dock to the house, hoping that the Canadian bush type of therapy would bring this nervous little space traveler back to us earth people.

Irving spent a week with us, and gradually, he slowed down, but not too much. We took him fishing, to get him away from the telephone for a few hours, and he seemed to relax, with the exception of every once in a while frantically jotting weird hieroglyphics between other mystic symbols on the backs of old envelopes. He even wrote a few things on the boat seats.

"What language do you use for your notes?" I asked.

He looked at me with the utmost disdain. "For a writer," he said, "you certainly have definite gaps in your education —long, deep gaps. Don't you recognize English?"

"I'm sorry," I said. "At Lynbrook High we only had basket weaving and bead stringing."

"Sounds like a pretty backward institution."

"*It* was—and *we* were. The first time we got a Negro in our class we were extremely puzzled. We thought he was a chocolate Italian."

"That reminds me"—Irving cast his rod wildly as if he intended beating the fish to death with the feathered fly—"I gotta call Sidney when we get back to the house."

"Who's Sidney?" Reiko said.

"Boy, you *do* live back in the bush, don'tcha? Sidney Poitier—he's the hottest thing since Sammy Davis, Jr."

"I *love* Sammy Davis," Reiko said.

"Yeah," said Irving. "But he never coulda done *Guess Who's Coming to Dinner.*"

"Why?" Reiko said. "He looks pretty *hungry!*"

Back at the house, Irving, who by this time was quite used to the difficulty we have in getting through to the mobile telephone operator in Chinookville, would still pick up the receiver with never-diminishing optimism. By some miracle, this time, he got through immediately, but unfortunately, Sidney Poitier was attending a white militant meeting and couldn't be reached.

Irving then decided not to lose his winning streak and tried to get Richard Burton in London. He got London, all right, but it was London, Ontario, and by the time this was discovered he had to contend with one Dion Desormeaux, who really dominated our fifteen-party line, because of his tenacity, plus no small dose of ferocity. Dion had a huge reservoir of invective with which he drowned any and all opposition to his private use of this fifteen-party line. Anyone who could stand up to this maniacal French Canadian, under other conditions would have been given a Purple Heart, plus the *Croix de guerre* and a merit badge for thick skin.

In Irving Laveeeene, Dion Desormeaux had met his match, and it shook him up. English profanity became mixed with French profanity to emerge as a wild blasphemous succotash, which was consumed, with obvious relish, by both parties.

"Look, you frog bastard," Irving said, "I'm trying to talk to Richard Burton in London—now get off the line!"

"I will not get off the line!" Dion Desormeaux bellowed. "Not for *you* or any other sonofabitchin' English, tea-sucking, bastardly, ball-breaking brass-ass!"

Listening in on our extension phone, I almost applauded this Pulitzer Prize adjective collection, but instead and quite inadvertently and because I wanted to know, I said, "What's a brass-ass?"

"Who was that?" Dion Desormeaux said.

"It was probably Richard Burton," Irving said. "Now will you get the hell off this phone?"

"What's a brass-ass?" I repeated.

"Well—" Dion Desormeaux said, seemingly hesitant about taking on another brass-ass.

"What's a brass-ass?" I insisted, now that his will to live was rapidly diminishing.

"A brass-ass, Mr. Burton," Dion Desormeaux began, in a voice which had changed from a high scream to a low whimper, quavering with genuflection, "is a sonofabitchin', tea-sucking, bastardly, ball-breaking Englishman, if you'll pardon the expression, Mr. Burton." Then he quietly hung up.

"Richard, is that you?" Irving said.

"No, it's Elizabeth," I said. "What the hell do you want? You know what *time* it is over here? *Brass-ass!*" Then *I* hung up.

"Just talked to Liz and Dickie," Irving said as he came back to the living room a moment later. "They're *wild* about the idea. Absolutely wild! Who needs Sidney Poitier!"

"Instead of Sidney Poitier, you're gonna use Richard Burton and Elizabeth Taylor?" I said.

"But of course," Irving said. "Who else could do it?"

"How about Paul Newman and Joanne Woodward?" I said.

"That's an idea," Irving agreed, pouring himself a large Alka-Seltzer and selecting three different colored tranquilizers from his extensive collection. "A very good idea."

"I like Phyllis Diller and Bob Hope," Reiko said from her nest in front of the fireplace.

"I like *Star Trek*," Bobby said.

"What is this great story that seems to be so perfect for so many people?" I said.

"It's a natural," Irving said. Then, in a voice trembling with emotion and reverence, he gestured with his hand, as if he were spelling it on a marquee: "The Day Jim Bishop Died." He hesitated for a moment—spellbound. Then he said with a confidence born of many failures, "How does that grab you?"

"How's it gonna grab Jim Bishop?" I said.

"Don't worry about him," Irving said. "He's only a writer."

"I never thought about it that way," I said.

"Would you like-a tea?" Reiko said, uncurling and stretching like Pussycat.

"I would like-a *Star Trek*," Bobby said.

"Bobby," I said, "stop making fun of your mother, and go get the worms—we're going fishing."

Toward the end of a week of the peace and tranquillity of Lost Lake, Irving was a raving maniac. The silence and inactivity had driven him to the edge of madness, but we were determined to hold him for the full seven days.

"Can't you forget business for a few days, Irving?" I said. "The way you're going you'll be in an early grave."

"I don't care where I am," he said. "As long as it's got a phone!"

"We've got a phone," Reiko said. "It cost forty-eight dollars a month."

"I mean a phone that connects to the outside world," Irving said. "There are *people* out there! Don't you realize that, you—you *tree dwellers!*"

"Irving," I said, "if you don't like it here, why don't you go someplace else, but forget about business for a while? Business isn't important if you haven't got your health. Why don't you go to—well, why don't you go to Greece? Athens is beautiful at this time of year."

"Athens is where you change planes for Tel Aviv," Irving snapped, "and that's *it.*"

"That's an idea," I said. "Why don't you go to Tel Aviv? It's lovely at this time of year."

"Tel Aviv is where you change planes for Athens!" he said, and selected three more shades of tranquilizers from the top shelf of his pillbox. Then he poured himself a triple shot of scotch to wash them down with.

"You're not supposed to mix tranquilizers with whiskey," I said.

Irving looked at me like nothing in the world would make him happier than to grab me by the neck and smash my skull against the wall.

"I read that in a *Peace* Corps handbook," I said, before he went into action. "Look, Irving, what about the Riviera? Monaco?"

"Naw," he said, almost normally, "Grace-baby don't wanna do no more movies. She digs that princess bit."

"There's always Acapulco," I said.

"Are you kidding?" he said. "After Merle Oberon, Dolores Del Rio and Las Brisas and going to the bathroom every twenty minutes—what have you got?"

"Maybe you could make a movie down there," I said.

"We know Dolores Del Rio," Reiko said. "She's now married to Louie Riley—Junior—and she's very happy, but maybe she'd like to make a movie."

"Yeah," I said, and using Irving's marquee gesture, I spelled it out: "The Day Acapulco Died—with Merle Oberon and Dolores Riley, Jr.—also starring Van Johnson and Moms Mabley—"

"I don't like Moms Mabley," Irving said, "not for the mother."

"Then we're back to Rod Steiger," I said.

"*I* see what you're trying to do," Irving said. "You're trying to get my mind off this terrible, remote, godforsaken wilderness, and you're keeping me here against my will. How could you do this to me, Jack? I've been your agent for twenty years—twenty long years. Isn't that true?"

"Yes," I admitted, "but in twenty long years you never got me a job."

"So what?" Irving said, swallowing more pills and more whiskey which he was now blending in a Waring Blender. "Doesn't loyalty count for *something?*"

"Not at the Montreal Mortgage and Loan Company," I said. "Or the A & P."

Irving just sighed and threw himself on the circular couch—in a dejected circle. "Writers!" he said. "They're all alike. And they don't know how to live. A party-line phone with *fourteen* other people! Imagine a thing like this going on right *now*—*here* in the *twenty-first century!*" Then the pills and the alcohol caught up with him and he lapsed into a peaceful coma.

17

IN my youth I wanted to take a hotel management course at Cornell University. The fact that I had never been in a hotel or graduated from high school seemed no deterrent at the time. Also I was then playing drums with Al Vann and his band and the $60 a week seemed a bit too much to give up just so I could run the Waldorf-Astoria. I thought maybe I could do it between sets, but Al said no. For $60 a week he "didn't want no moonlighting!"

The transition from my youthful ambitions, while beating the skins for a living, to a sudden inspiration—thirty years later in the wilds of Canada—seemed logical and simple enough. To me. We owned what would be termed in many places—a village. A village of empty houses. Why couldn't we turn Lost Lake into a refuge for the jet set? A haven for those who had had enough of Davos, Acapulco, St.-Tropez, Capri, and Snowmass?

Reiko was enthusiastic about the idea because it meant seeing people again, which, she admitted, might be a change. I wasn't too sure of *my* cordiality in this respect. You can't have a resort *without people*, although I think it would be a giant step in the right direction.

Actually, the idea for some kind of commercial use of our vacant cabins was suggested by a friend, Alan Schwartz, a professor at Iona College in New Rochelle, who was visiting us. Professor Schwartz suggested we rent the cabins to *writers* and make our nonpaying compound into something that would help with the $97-a-year land tax. "Writers," he said, "would love to find a place like this to write."

"Harold Robbins does all his writing on the Riviera," I said.

"What does *he* know?" he said. "He's a millionaire."

"I never thought of it that way," I said. "But how many writers do you think we could get up here to make enough to pay the ninety-seven dollars?"

"How many empty cabins you got?" the professor said.

"When you leave, we'll have seven," I said.

"I don't wanna leave," he said.

"What about Iona College?" I said. "Don't you want to stay there until you're old and endearing like Mr. Chips?"

"Yeah," he said. "Maybe they'll write a book about me, *Good-bye, Mr. Schwartz.*"

"You won't have to get old and endearing," I said. "It'll be good-bye, Mr. Schwartz, if you don't get back there by next Monday." He looked crushed, so I said, "If you want to stay, we'll only have six cabins to rent to writers, but it's okay. Six writers is plenty. It's a lucky number—six."

"Since when?" he said.

"Since just now. This is my island, and I can make any number lucky."

"Well—Salaam! Salaam!" he said. "Why don't you proclaim yourself king and rent out your cabins to princes?"

"How about princesses?"

"Now you're talkin' sense," he said. "Get Monaco on the phone and don't talk to anyone but Gracie."

"The last time I called Monaco," I said, "I got Tony Curtis."

"His real name is Bernie Schwartz," Alan Schwartz said.

"What's *your* real name," I said.

"Alan Curtis. I changed it to Schwartz when I started teaching at Iona."

"I don't understand," I said. "Iona is a Catholic college."

"Right," he said.

"Why didn't you change your name to O'Brian?"

"O'Brian Schwartz?"

This went on for some time. I think we both had cabin fever, which is something you get if you're in the bush too long. Or in *anything* too long.

The first step in our switch from a hermitage to a swinging, successfully populated summer and winter resort was to put an ad in the New York papers. We put one in each of the three survivors, the New York *Times,* the *Daily News,* and the *Post.* The copy in the ads, which Alan and I cooked up ourselves, was aimed at the intellectual, with money, who wanted to get away from it all. We emphasized the pristine wilderness side of everything and soft-pedaled the sports aspect. We stressed the *après*-ski activities heavily, because there was no skiing. We hinted that après-ski might be our *only* activity, which we felt would have a universal appeal to AA dropouts in general and nonathletes in particular. We tried to give the impression that we wished to cater to bums with money. Also we didn't feel we should encourage families who had close ties with their pubescent offspring. The children could stay home with relatives or could be settled in an all-night movie house for a week or so with a gunny sack of peanut butter sandwiches and instructions not to sit next to any dirty old men with their flies open. Or dirty old ladies in the same condition.

The response to our advertising campaign was overwhelming from families *with children* who wanted to go *skiing.*

Proving once again that although the United States is an extremely literate area (compared to Micronesia), nobody understands what they read, because they read too fast, or they read into what they read something else besides what they are reading. That's what Gertrude Stein used to say—only more clearly.

The first family to arrive at the Lost Lake Inn (which we now called it) were the Digby Potters. They were from Boston and they'd never been farther north than the Old North Church.

Mr. and Mrs. Potter arrived with three children ranging in ages from four to seventeen. The seventeen child was an extremely attractive, squirmy, pouty, and spoiled girl. The middle-sized one was an eight-year-old boy who looked like he had been smoking pot since he was three. He looked like Attila the Hun with Shirley Temple's dimples. When I said, "How are you, son?" he said, "If I was *your* son, I'd cut my throat!" Then he whipped out a switchblade knife with an eight-inch blade and six notches on the handle. I didn't ask about the notches.

"Randolf," Mrs. Potter said. "How many times have I told you? Stop waving that knife around. You'll just start trouble—Stanley will want one, too." Then she patted four-year-old Stanley on top of his bright-red head, and Stanley promptly began screaming.

"You see," Mrs. Potter said.

"I came up here to relax!" Mr. Potter said; then he cuffed Randolf with an Air Canada tote bag which must have contained a bowling ball, because Randolf's head ricocheted back off the $5 worth of bubble gum he had in his mouth. He promptly assumed a low crouch, holding the switchblade as if he was in *West Side Story*. I thought Papa Potter's large intestine was going to be festooned all over the dock like a street dance in Venice, but Papa Potter gave little Randolf a backhander with the same tote bag and restored order, if not equanimity, in the little group.

Little Stanley was still screaming, but he was having difficulty in making himself heard over Chibi, the Malemute, Tanuki the wolf's howling, plus Doggie's yapping and Bobby's bugling. (In a moment fraught with insanity we had bought him this charming musical instrument, thinking it would be therapeutic.)

"I came up here to *relax!*" Papa Potter shrieked from his foam-flecked mouth, swinging his bowling ball at Bobby's head, but Bobby, having learned to duck at a very early age, avoided concussion neatly and continued to play what he thought was "Alexander's Ragtime Band" at a safer distance.

"Relax, Digby," commanded Mrs. Potter. I thought for a moment, after she said this, *she* would be getting a taste of the bowling ball, but Digby thought better of it. Maybe she carried a switchblade, too.

Charlie Burke, the pilot, who had brought them to the lake, jumped back onto the port pontoon, and shoved the Beaver away from the dock, at the same time making conversation like, "Say, Jack, seen any more rattlesnakes lately?"

"No," I said, "but two grizzlies attacked us yesterday when we were picking blueberries."

"You have *all* the fun!" Charlie shouted from the drifting plane.

The Potter family stood like frozen statues during this pleasant exchange; then suddenly Mrs. Potter exploded. "Rattlesnakes! Grizzlies! Get that plane back! *Get . . . that . . . plane . . . back!*"

The plane was well away from the dock, and Charlie had started the engine and was taxiing rapidly toward the opposite end of the lake.

"You don't *hafta* pick blueberries," Bobby said, then swung into "I found my thrill on Blueberry Hill" on his bugle.

"If that kid doesn't stop blowin' that thing," shouted Mr. Potter, "I'll saw off his lips!"

"Please, Papa," Randolf said, "I came up here to *relax!*"

Papa Potter swung his bowling ball once more and Randolf relaxed. A bit too much, I thought.

It took Reiko and me a long forty-five minutes to convince the Potters that there were no rattlesnakes or grizzlies in our vicinity. By this time Jake, who had been promoted from idiot to bellboy, had been standing by to help with the luggage. When I called, "Front, boy!" he closed his eyes and leaned precariously against a slim birch at the water's edge. I yelled again, but nothing happened. I thought: *He's cooked up a new ailment—sleeping sickness!*

"Papa," Bobby said, between requests, "why don't you cut down that little tree? Then he'll fall into the lake. That ought to wake him up."

"Your father is against the pollution of our natural resources," I said.

"What does that mean?"

"Forget it," I said. "Blow your bugle." Then I stepped close to one of Jake's pointed ears and shouted loud and clear, "How about a martini?" This did it. Our un-Admirable Crichton was instantly with the living again. I then said, "Jake, take Mr. and Mrs. Potter and their children to Honeymoon Heaven."

"What the hell's that?" he said.

"The last cabin on the left, you dumb bastard," I stage-whispered in a stage whisper that could be heard as far west as Winnipeg. Jake had never heard me use my Prussian field marshal's voice before, and before he realized what he was doing, he picked up the seventeen pieces of Potter luggage and staggered off on a trot to Honeymoon Heaven with the Potter family trailing him unenthusiastically.

As soon as they were out of earshot, Reiko said, "I don't think it's a very good idea."

"What's not a very good idea?" I said, knowing perfectly well what wasn't a very good idea.

"Those . . . people. I think we're going to have trouble," she said.

"What kinda trouble?"

"They won't like it here."

"Why not?"

"They would like Las Vegas better," Reiko said.

"Las Vegas!" I said. "Then why in the hell didn't they go there? Mr. Potter wants to relax. That's why they came here."

"Maybe so," Reiko said, "but Mrs. Potter doesn't want to relax, and neither does that girl or that Stanley or that Randolf—you'll see."

I did see. About seven minutes later Mrs. Potter came storming toward the main lodge, her voluminous bosoms rising and falling like the Bay of Fundy as she panted up the stone walk. I could see through my peephole in the drapes that she was not happy. She didn't bother with knocking and that was her mistake because just about then Reiko had decided to let Pussycat run around the house for a while. As the door slammed open, Pussycat sprang up to the lowest beam like a rocket and hung there, snarling and spitting. I thought she overdid it, but with a 150-pound cougar, the best policy is love, not war, so I didn't try to admonish the dear thing. Mrs. Potter stood in the doorway, not knowing whether to scream, or run, or dampen her dainty drawers. It didn't take her long to simultaneously do all three. I gave her a few minutes; then I walked over to Honeymoon Heaven. The closer I got, the louder she got. I've never heard a woman with such strident head tones. All the fish I'm sure were huddled together in a frightened circle at the north end of the lake like cattle in a blizzard, wondering if they could make it over the beaver dam and to the safety of *another* lake. *I* toyed with the idea of *another* lake, too. Maybe some lake with no exits and no entrances and no record of it on any map.

I kicked, timidly, on the door of Honeymoon Heaven with the toe of my lumberjack boot. Mrs. Potter reached the top of her crescendo, and communication with her through the closed door I felt was going to be difficult, if not impossible, so I opened it, and said, "Evenin', folks, how y'all," just like Kay Kyser used to, back in the old radio days. Mrs. Potter, the squirmy pouty daughter, Randolf, and Stanley looked at me like I was Happy Harry, your friendly neighborhood hangman.

"I just wanna relax," Mr. Potter said from his comfy bed and with his comfy bottle of Pinch and his comfy boozed-up smile.

"Shut up, Digby!" Mrs. Potter said, baring a full six inches of canine tooth. "Mr. Douglas," she said, turning her winning ways abruptly on me, "Mr. Douglas, what was that animal in your living room?"

"Oh," I said. "That was Pussycat."

"A pussycat! That snarling, vicious, wild, spitting beast was a pussycat?"

"No," I explained, "it's a cougar, but we call her Pussycat."

"God Almighty!" Mrs. Potter said. "That's like calling a man-eating shark Fishy."

"Well, they are a little," I said.

"I'm hungry," Stanley said, and Randolf said the same thing.

"I'm startin' to relax," Mr. Potter said, as his elbow

knocked his bottle of scotch off the night table with a glassy crash.

"What time is dinner served?" Mrs. Potter said, starting to regain some of what passed for poise at Bryn Mawr.

"Suit yourself," I said. "The cookshack is right over there next to the laundry cabin."

"I beg your pardon," Mrs. Potter said.

"The cookshack," I said. "It's that cabin right over there. It's really two rooms. The kitchen and the bathroom."

"That's very interesting," Mrs. Potter said, allowing a Radcliffe chest tone to escape through her flawless Bostonian glottis. "I'm sure a tour of the kitchen would be most instructive and entertaining—I shall wear my white gloves— but what I'm trying to find out is: What time do you serve dinner? And where is the dining room?"

"I don't serve dinner," I said. "Reiko does. And we usually eat on a coffee table in front of the fire."

"That sounds very comfy-cozy," Mr. Potter said, popping himself another pop from a fresh bottle of Pinch. "An open fire, a jug of wine and thou," Mr. Potter continued. "You know who said that?"

"You did, Papa," little Stanley said. Papa gave little Stanley a long hard look. Then offered him a drink.

"Mr. Douglas," Mrs. Potter said, "there are certain things my husband can't eat."

"Whatever he can't eat," I said, "just save it, and I'll take it over and give it to the bears."

"I don't understand what you're talking about," Mrs. Potter said. "There are certain kinds of food I don't want him to have."

Stubbornly, I resisted what she was saying, although I knew the inevitable was about to happen. The culinary moment of truth was near. I wanted to be gentle and kind, because I had taken gentle and kind lessons from the Famous Westport School of Compassion, but somehow, in this moment of confrontation, I forgot the whole course, so I said, like a governor denying the condemned's plea for commutation after the switch has been thrown, "Mrs. Potter, you cook whatever you like for dinner, and afterward, if you want to watch the hockey game or *The Glenn Miller Story* on TV, come on over to our house."

The way Mrs. Potter looked at me I thought she was going to ask Randolf for his switchblade.

"You mean—*I* have to cook?" she said.

"Yes."

"What am I gonna cook?"

"You didn't bring any supplies?" I said.

"What the hell is this?" she said. "What do you mean—supplies? What are we paying a hundred dollars a week apiece for?"

"Relaxation," Mr. Potter said, comfy-dozily.

"Mrs. Potter," I said, echoing Paul Newman, "what we have here seems to be a lack of communication. In our brochure the whole thing is carefully spelled out. For a hundred dollars a week you are entitled to a cabin and kitchen privileges, and you must bring your own food, or we can have it flown in."

"That sounds like fun," Mr. Potter said to his wife. "Let's have some ham and eggs fly in from 21."

"Shut up!" Mrs. Potter suggested.

"Not many wild stallions left," I said, remembering a line from an old Marlboro commercial.

"What?" Mrs. Potter whirled on me.

"Oh," I said, "I was just trying to get your mind off your problem. I was trying to divert you."

"Get that plane back here," Mrs. Potter snarled, "and get it back quick. We're going to leave this—this do-it-yourself madhouse—with a cougar in the living room and no food for the paying guests! I'm going to write to my Congressman about this!"

"You'd better write to your member of Parliament—this is Canada, y'know."

"Well, I don't know what I'm going to do or who I'm going to turn to," Mrs. Potter said, then changed gears into a yell, "but they'd better start fortifying that border! That's all I've got to say!"

Mr. Potter propped himself up on one elbow and looked at his wife; then he said, "There—you see—everybody is starting to relax already."

"You're drunk!" Mrs. Potter said. "Children, don't look."

"Papa's funny when he's stoned," Randolf said.

"Yeah—stoned," Stanley said.

"That's the only time he's funny," the squirmy, pouty seventeen-year-old daughter said.

"What about the plane?" Mrs. Potter said.

"I can't get it back tonight," I said. "It's getting dark, and they can't land in the dark."

"Can't you wave a flashlight or something?"

"No," I said, "it would disturb the bats."

After I said this, Mrs. Potter backed away from me, closely toward the bed and her husband; she reached behind her without looking and picked up the whiskey bottle and took a long slug from it. Then she set it down behind her and said, "I've never disturbed a bat in my life and I'm not going to start in now."

The Potters were with us for the next three days, because the next three days were the foggiest three days in the history of Upper Canada, and nothing was flying—except Mr. Potter. We couldn't take our reluctant guests into Chinookville by Land Rover because the rain had soaked the timber road into a soggy, bottomless mess.

The foggiest three days in the history of Upper Canada also became the longest three days. The squirmy, pouty seventeen-year-old Potter daughter became progressively poutier and squirmier.

"She needs a good hump," Jake said, making sense for the first time in his life.

Mrs. Potter absolutely refused to enter the cookshack—mainly because she had nothing to cook—so Reiko graciously volunteered, but because we ate many Japanese dishes, her efforts were not too well received. These proper Bostonians just couldn't get used to soy sauce on their bean and their cod—and their tapioca pudding. But although they didn't complain, they ate silently and sullenly, like bloody but unbowed political prisoners around the festive board on Devil's Island—on a rainy Christmas Eve.

When the Potters were not sitting in front of our fireplace reluctantly keeping themselves alive, their paths never crossed. Mr. Potter, who had neglected to bring food to Lost Lake, hadn't forgotten the other necessities—like scotch, bourbon, gin, vodka, rum, rye, tequila, brandy, elderberry wine, and a dirty glass. The dirty glass he kept pencils in to write postcards to the folks back home telling them what a good time he was having and X marked his room.

I had managed to sneak the switchblade knife away from dear Randolf before he could use it on Bobby, but with Randolf unarmed, Bobby took advantage of the situation and suddenly displayed a side to his character of which Reiko and I were unaware. We hadn't realized we had been harboring an incipient nihilist, until Randolf grabbed one of Bobby's Matchbox cars and Bobby reacted instantly by slashing Randolf on the head with a wooden samurai sword. If it had been the genuine article, Randolf would have come out twins. Randolf ran screaming toward Honeymoon Heaven with Bobby in hot pursuit. Mrs. Potter dashed to the aid of her whelp, who she thought was being hunted to the death by Pussycat and Tanuki. She screamed to her husband, "Digby! The cougar and the wolf are loose!" Mr. Potter coasted through the open doorway of Honeymoon Heaven, sizing up the situation as best he could with his blood-shot eyes losing the battle to focus. All he could see was Randolf, with a sizable lump growing larger on his forehead clinging to his mother's bottom and Bobby standing there, uncertainly, with his little samurai sword.

"Where's the cougar and the wolf?" Mr. Potter demanded.

"They're over in the pen," Bobby said, indicating the huge chain-like fenced area.

"Good," Mr. Potter said; then he turned to his wife and smiled a little crooked Paul Lynde smile. "You know something, Gladys—I'm beginning to like it here. I'm really starting to unwind." Then he did a passable about-face and zigzagged back into the cabin.

"I'm sorry this happened, Mrs. Potter," I said, still a little breathless. "Bobby, you mustn't hit people with that sword! Ranger Rick wouldn't do that."

"Oh?" Bobby said. "How would *he* kill *him?*"

He pointed at Randolf, who left the safety of his mother's bottom and asked warily, "Who's Ranger Rick?"

"He's a raccoon," I said.

"Raccoon?" Mrs. Potter said.

"Yes."

"Friend of yours?"

"He's everybody's friend," Bobby said. "Isn't that right, Papa?"

"Yeah," I said, trying to sound sane.

"Ranger Rick tells a lot of funny stories, doesn't he, Papa?" Bobby said.

"Yeah," I said.

Mrs. Potter pushed her Randolf back a little so he would be within handy grabbing distance of her bottom and said, "This raccoon tells a lot of funny stories?"

"Yes," I said. "You see, Ranger Rick is connected with the National Wildlife Federation and—"

Mrs. Potter cut in quickly. "I'll *bet* he is!"

"Wait a minute," I said. "You don't understand. You see, Ranger Rick puts out this magazine and—"

"You mean this raccoon is a publisher—of a magazine?"

"No. You see—"

Mrs. Potter chopped me off short with: "Mr. Douglas, if this fog doesn't lift soon, I am going to start walking back to civilization. I refuse to believe *any* of this—because if I *did*, I would have to request to be put away in an institution, because I would be as crazy as everybody *else* connected with this whole mad setup is!"

Then she left Bobby and me standing there, slamming the door to Honeymoon Heaven so hard all the little pink plastic fornicating cupids along the doorframe became unglued.

"Ranger Rick is my favorite raccoon," Bobby said, taking my hand, as we walked back to our house.

"Yeah," I said. "Mine, too."

"Next time," Bobby said, "let's tell Mrs. Potter about Jimmy Stink, the skunk."

"Yeah," I said, "and don't forget Rudy, the red-nosed rattlesnake. She tells some pretty funny stories, too."

Then there's Gore Vidal.

Of All Brands Sold: Lowest tar: 2 mg. "tar," 0.2 mg. nicotine av. per cigarette, FTC Report Apr. 1976. **Kent Golden Lights Menthol:** 8 mg. "tar," 0.7 mg. nicotine av. per cigarette by FTC Method.

KENT GOLDEN LIGHTS MENTHOL.
LOWER IN TAR THAN ALL THESE MENTHOL BRANDS.

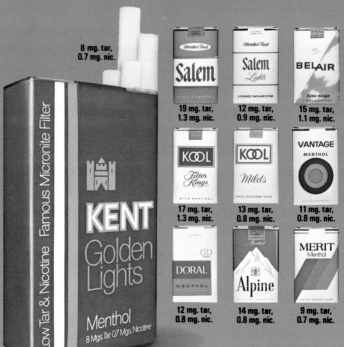

8 mg. tar, 0.7 mg. nic.

Salem — 19 mg. tar, 1.3 mg. nic.

Salem Lights — 12 mg. tar, 0.9 mg. nic.

BELAIR Filter Kings Light Menthol — 15 mg. tar, 1.1 mg. nic.

KOOL Filter Kings Mild Menthol — 17 mg. tar, 1.3 mg. nic.

KOOL Milds — 13 mg. tar, 0.8 mg. nic.

VANTAGE MENTHOL — 11 mg. tar, 0.8 mg. nic.

DORAL MENTHOL — 12 mg. tar, 0.8 mg. nic.

Alpine — 14 mg. tar, 0.8 mg. nic.

MERIT Menthol — 9 mg. tar, 0.7 mg. nic.

KENT Golden Lights Menthol 8 Mgs. Tar 0.7 Mgs. Nicotine
Low Tar & Nicotine · Famous Micronite Filter

REAL MENTHOL REFRESHMENT AT ONLY 8 MG TAR.

© Lorillard, U.S.A., 1976

16	**13**	**13**	**13**	**11**	**9**
MG TAR	MG TAR	MG TAR	MG TAR	MG TAR	MG TAR
0.9 mg. nic.	0.9 mg. nic.	0.8 mg. nic.	0.9 mg. nic.	0.7 mg. nic.	0.7 mg. nic.

STILL SMOKING MORE TAR THAN YOU HAVE TO TO GET GOOD TASTE?

ONLY 8 mg tar

TASTE KENT GOLDEN LIGHTS.

Of All Brands Sold: Lowest tar: 2 mg. "tar," 0.2 mg. nicotine av. per cigarette, FTC Report Apr. 1976. **Kent Golden Lights:** 8 mg. "tar," 0.7 mg. nicotine av. per cigarette by FTC Method.

Warning: The Surgeon General Has Determined That Cigarette Smoking Is Dangerous to Your Health.

18

ONE morning, in late November, Jake was sitting in our living room, wondering what he was going to do with himself all day for the $16 I was paying him for that day.

"Why don't you cut some firewood?" I helpfully suggested, aiming an automatic rifle at his head (mentally).

"Don't seem like just the right day to cut firewood," Jake said.

"How come?" I said. "You've been telling me right along that the best time to cut firewood was when it got cold. Well, it got cold."

"Yeah," he said, "it *did* get cold." I thought that was the end of it there in the bush, and our next step might have to be the UN, when Jake volunteered that he had cut enough firewood to last us all winter and he had it cached all around the lake at various convenient locations.

"Maybe you'd better show me the various convenient locations," I said, "just in case you're sick or something when we need firewood." Already I was laying the ground for getting rid of this not so Artful Dodger and supplanting him with someone who wasn't shot full of every kind of ache, pain, pox, and mortification and to whom labor was not a stupefying experience to be endured for as little time as possible.

"Don't seem like just the right day to show you the various convenient locations of your winter supply of wood," he said, tapping his diaphragm, trying to arrange for some itinerant gas in his stomach to rise.

"Why?"

The gas rose, and after Jake had lowered himself back

113

down in my easy chair, he said, "Because it's going to snow. Yeah, that's it—it's going to snow!"

"When?"

"Tonight."

"Well, then," I said, "that gives us all day to scout out the convenient locations." There was a horrible silence after this, during which Jake used a divining rod to locate some more gas. He found some, and he and the gas rose at the same time, and twenty minutes later we were in one of the boats heading for the first of the convenient birch caches, which was at the south end of the lake around in back of a huge outcropping of what looked like basalt to me. A beaver slapped his tail on the water's surface and dived out of sight as we glided into the cove past two huge beaver houses.

"The sonsabitches!" said Jake.

"The beavers?" I said. "What did they do now?"

"No," he said. "Not the beavers—them goddamn campers! They used up all the firewood. It was right over there. That's where I stacked it. Right over there." He pointed to a small peninsula, which from the look of it, had never felt the tread of man or heard the sound of a chain saw. It looked to me like it must have looked to the Hurons who inhabited this area a hundred years ago.

"Where did you cut the wood?" I said, trying to sound like Perry Mason, or Christine Jorgenson when she forgets herself.

"Right over there," he said, pointing to a virgin stand of yellow birch, "I cut about six cords."

He had been nowhere near this place, so I said, "Well, let's just forget about this place. Those campers sure must have been cold to use that much wood."

"Sonsabitches!" he said.

"Yeah," I said, "lotta sonsabitches in this world—especially when it comes to stealing firewood. J. Edgar Hoover says that that's the number one crime in the United States—it comes right after buggery."

Jake was pretty quiet after I said this. He might have been more sensitive than I thought.

"Show me where else there's firewood stacked," I said. "And I hope it's well hidden."

"Oh, it is," he said. "I took special precautions after I found out that this stack was gone."

"Oh," I said, "you *knew* that this stack had been stolen?"

"Oh, sure," he said, "I check this whole lake out all the time. I know what's going on every minute."

"Uh-huh," I said. "Then what were we looking for back there in the cove—fingerprints?"

Jake ignored this completely and steered the boat toward the north end of the lake. We cruised past the place where we fed the bears and passed two tiny pine-spiked islands and into another cove. Jake cut the outboard motor, and we slid silently into the stillness of the little bay. A marten—or maybe it was a fisher that had been eyeing us with great curiosity—decided to beat a hasty retreat and ran along the branches from tree to tree with tremendous speed and agility. When he got closer to the land, Jake suddenly said, "The sonsabitches! Those goddamn sonsabitches!"

"Those campers again, huh?" I said.

"Yeah," he said, "the sonsabitches stole every goddamn cord of wood I cut and stacked right over there under that big tamarack!"

"I don't see any tamarack," I said.

"Those crummy punks!" he said. "Don't tell me they took that, too!"

"If you're talking about that big dark tree there, that's a hemlock."

"Oh, yeah," he said, "I forgot to bring my tree glasses. I'm wearin' my firewood glasses."

"Where's the next convenient location of stacked firewood that we are going to use this winter?"

"Not far," Jake said, "not far." He started the outboard motor once again and skillfully maneuvered the little boat over some treacherous rocks that only gouged a few small holes in the bow and broke the shear pin off the propeller shaft.

"Oh, fudge!" Jake said, trying to impress me with his control under stress. "I didn't bring any extra shear pins or a pair of pliers."

"I did," I said, and handed him a shear pin and the pliers. I hadn't been reading the *Popular Outboard Motor* magazine all these years for nothing. After we were once again on the way, we passed the "Doctor's Island" and headed into still another cove. Again Jake cut the motor, and we glided noiselessly through the green-blue water toward a large rock shelf. I beat him to it this time. "The sonsabitches!" I said.

"Whatsamatter?" Jake said, startled.

"There's no firewood stacked on the shore—those goddamn campers!"

"How do you know?" Jake said.

"I don't," I said. "But this job has all the earmarks of the others. The MO is exactly the same!"

"Yeah," Jake said, "the same MO."

"I tell you what you do, Jake," I said. "The rest of the day you cut firewood and I'll keep my eye out for sonsabitches. OK?"

Jake thought about this. Then he said, "My ulcer's startin' to act up."

"Mine, too," I said, unsheathing my brand-new hunting knife with the six-inch blade and running my finger along its edge.

Jake almost dislocated his elbow getting the motor started on the first pull.

19

AFTER we had moved permanently into our new northern Canadian home, we had to have some work done on it to make it warm enough for us to withstand the 40 and 50 below zero temperatures. This actually wasn't too cold compared with other parts of the world. Tanana, Alaska, had had a record of 76 below and a place called Snag, in the Yukon, once got down to 81 below, which is really not bad compared to 126 below zero in Vostok, Antarctica. Incidentally, why hasn't Bob Hope or Billy Graham or Mamie Van Doren visited these places at Christmastime? They're *starved* for entertainment!

But getting back to home improvement, bush style. First, I hired a carpenter who had been recommended by a friend, but this friend warned me that this carpenter, although he was a good worker, was tricky and had to be watched at all times. This worthy, whom I shall call Clyde, in turn hired two other carpenters to help him. We could not be there for the first two weeks they were working because we were up at the northern tip of Quebec taking movies of Indians, but I felt that this wasn't taking too much of a risk, because I had not paid them anything in advance.

The first week had been spent, we learned later, in dragging all the necessary lumber, nails, roofing paper, shingles, and other supplies down the timber road to Lost Lake. A feat which could only be compared to Hannibal's getting his impedimenta over the Alps. Both were logistic impossibilities. But somehow it was accomplished. This Herculean task slowed somewhat the progress I had been led to anticipate from Clyde on winterizing our new home, and I was disappointed, when we finally arrived, to find that the double roof, which I expected to be completely finished, was hardly begun.

After our plane had landed and was floating into the dock, and after the initial disillusion (roof-wise), I saw what might be a girl amid the male trio who were standing with their hands on their hips, waiting for the rubber bumpers to zunk into the dock, which was Charlie Burke's cue to yell, "Lost Lake! Last stop! All out!" The girl, whom I shall call Bonnie, was like no female I had ever seen before, even while barnstorming with Woody Herman's Herd, through the coal-mining towns of Pennsylvania.

When we stumbled down the precarious rungs and out of the plane, she smiled at us. This is a supposition. She rolled back her lipstick-flaked *labia majora* and revealed three Ultra-Brite teeth: two upper canines and one lower central incisor. She looked like a muskrat trap. She smiled again and ran her talons through her hair, which resembled nothing more than dyed Brillo. Then she smiled at Bobby; this time it was a special smile for children, which made her look like a retarded lizard. Bobby started to cry. But if you could ignore her facial irregularities, which took some doing, you would become aware of her breasts, which were the most fantastic mammary monuments I have ever seen. They were enormous, high, and pointed.

"This is Bonnie," Clyde said. "She's here . . . cooking for us," he continued, indicating, I thought, her unbelievable frontal achievements.

Reiko, who is no dope, quickly said, "I only eat Japanese food. And so does Bobby and Jack's on a diet."

"I had Japanese food once," said Bonnie. "Remember, Clyde—at the Chink's on West Street?"

"Yeah," said Clyde.

Remembering suddenly that I was a gentleman, if not a scholar, I said, "It's very nice of you to stay here and cook for the fellers, but it must get pretty lonely."

"Yeah," Bonnie said, rearranging her bosoms so there was only one on each side, "I like *Chink* food, too."

Careful not to turn our backs on this harpy, we dragged our suitcases and cameras to the lodge. "I'm worried," said Reiko. "Is she gonna use our kitchen?"

"I wouldn't wanna *stop* her," I said.

"And what about the *bathroom?*" Reiko said. "Is she gonna use *that*, too?"

"Relax," I said, "she's not gonna use your toothbrush. *That's* a cinch!"

"Is she going to *sit* on our toilet?" said Reiko.

"I hope so," I said. "She's a little cross-eyed, I wouldn't want her to try any trick shots."

"That's *funny*, Papa," Bobby said.

"Papa used to be a comedian."

"I know. What happened?"

"I married Mama; then I didn't feel so funny anymore."

"That's *funny!*" said Bobby.

"I don't want her sitting on my toilet," said Reiko.

"What are we gonna do about it?" I said. "She's probably been sitting on it for the past two weeks."

Reiko stopped unpacking and stood, puzzled, a pair of double-thick red thermal long drawers trailing the floor. "What do you mean—sitting on the toilet for two weeks?"

"I didn't mean continuously!"

"What's 'continuously'?"

I felt myself being sucked down in the quicksand of the

language barrier, but I didn't quit. "Continuously means all the time."

"That Bonnie was sitting on our toilet *all* the *time* for *two weeks!*"

"No," I said.

"I don't want her sitting on it at all," Reiko said, carefully folding the red underwear and putting it back in her suitcase. "Let her go out behind a tree. That's what people do in Japan."

"But this is Canada," I said.

"Then it's better," she said. "Lotsa more trees."

At that moment, Miss Three Fang tangoed through the front door and into the kitchen, explaining, "Time for their coffee break." Then proceeded to cook a seven-course snack.

Before long we discovered that the cook was only eighteen years old and was the girlfriend of Clyde. How convenient that she could cook, we thought. And how convenient for Clyde camping up here in the north woods with his very own sleeping bag. Bonnie and Clyde shared our best guest cabin, of course, which didn't make us jump for joy, but we figured what the hell—they wouldn't be here forever. Bill and Sandy, the other two men, shared another guest cabin.

Everything went smoothly for exactly two days. Or to put it more exactly until payday, which came on a Sunday night. I got out my checkbook or, to be more Canadian, *cheque-book*, and Bonnie got out her timebook. She was not only a cook and bed warmer, but a timekeeper and a bookkeeper and, as I very shortly found out, a very good provider for the little town of Kerry, Ontario, where almost everybody was a relative of hers.

First, I made out the paychecks for the men, and it was then I felt that things weren't exactly true-blue because there was a great disparity in the hours the men were supposed to have worked. Clyde, the boss, according to his Wesson-oil-soaked alabaster goddess' timebook, had put in 132 hours in the week just past. We had been there for two of those days, so that meant he had put in 26 hours a day for the five days previously. Gad! What a man! Bill and Sandy hadn't put in anywhere near this kind of time. Again, according to the Ava Gardner of the sweaty socks set.

I wrote these checks like a little soldier because I felt that being 116 miles back in the bush, Reiko and Bobby and I couldn't really start too much trouble with a pride of north woods brutes and a three-toothed sloth den mother.

Now came the expenses incurred for the Douglas project. The highlights were: $187 to Bonnie's father, Purdy Cassidy, for something called "transportation." By this time I knew we were in a very tight little trap, so I kept writing. $312 plus for groceries for eleven days. This grocery list was dated every other day, which was rather a dead giveaway, because someone who lives 116 miles back in the bush just does not go to town every day for groceries, and Bonnie could not drive a car, and Bill and Sandy could not either, so that left Clyde—and if he was driving back and forth to town every other day, how could he have put in that grueling 132 hours?

After the grocery bill came endless items such as: $14 Tom Cassidy (a brother) for "provision assistance" (I didn't ask about this). $56 Serge Cassidy (another brother) for "transportation of firewood" (I didn't ask about this either. I didn't think it wise when we had had ten cords of birch stacked near the kitchen door for months). $94 for three new tires for the Land Rover—check payable to Cassidy's Garage in Kerry. $43 to Cassidy Fuel Company for stove oil. $305 to the Cassidy Boat and Canoe Company for one Evinrude 7½-HP outboard motor. When I had the temerity to ask about this, Bonnie explained that the old (last year's) one had suddenly refused to run anymore and they felt they needed this new motor, even though we had eight other motors to choose from in the boathouse. I was about to protest when Bonnie smiled at me and I knew if I raised even one small voice, I would have been immediately eaten—mukluks and all.

As the evening wore on, we came to the final item on her list—I must make a check out to the cook for $175 for two weeks.

"What cook?" I said.

"Me," said Bonnie.

"Oh, I thought you were—" I didn't finish the sentence. I couldn't. I was crying. Bonnie was suddenly full of compassion. She wrote the check for me. And helped me sign it.

The next morning things were different. The moment we got up there was a Canada Goose Airways plane at the dock, and without even our coffee or good-byes we took off and flew directly to the bank in Chinookville and stopped payment on all the checks. The Cassidy dynasty was out of business forever. I felt like I was shutting down the Ponderosa. Or closing the Rescue Mission. I felt good.

The whole thing had generated in Reiko, whose sense of fair play had never been surpassed, a great head of Japanese steam, and immediately after we planed back to camp, she stormed, all five feet of her, into the kitchen, where Bonnie was preparing crepes suzette and cherries jubilee for the crew's coffee break.

"*Get out!*" said Reiko to Bonnie. "Go get your *thing* and *get out!*" What "thing" she never explained, but Bonnie, obviously shattered by Reiko's 90-pound fury, got out. Leaving a trail of cooking sherry and Aunt Jemima pancake batter. Then Reiko rushed outside again to where Clyde, strangely—all by himself—was hammering desultorily while standing near the top of a very weak ladder.

"Get out," Reiko screamed, "get out now. We send your stuff later!" Clyde was instantly on the ground, missing all but one rung on his way down.

"What's the matter?" he said.

"Don't ask question!" Reiko said. "Just go—and take Bill and Sandy, too."

"I fired them this morning," he said.

"What was that?" I said, coming out from behind the stacked cordwood, where I had been hiding from Reiko. I thought she might order me out, too. Such was the violence of her scathing anger.

"I fired Sandy and Bill this morning," Clyde said, a few decibels lower, now that he found himself surrounded. "They didn't want to work."

"You mean they didn't want to work a hundred and thirty-two hours a week, like you did last week?"

"That's it," this weasel said. "I believe a man should work an honest day's work if he expects an honest day's pay."

"Then why isn't the new roof on like it's supposed to be?"

"I just toldja—Bill and Sandy goofed off. *I* was the only one working."

"Where are they now," said Reiko, "if you fire them? How did they get out of the bushes?"

"They walked, I guess," Clyde said, with a slightly nervous sniggle. I wanted to shoot this bastard down right then and there, but I wasn't too sure of Canada's game laws.

At that moment Bonnie rushed up dragging a heavy suitcase. Reiko astounded me by grabbing Bonnie's suitcase and shouting, "Get out! Go get in the plane, and get out!"

"My suitcase!" pleaded Bonnie.

"We'll send it later," said Reiko. "After we look through it, we send it. You are very dishonest people!"

Bonnie and Clyde hurried toward the dock, and just as they reached it, Clyde hesitated and turned back to look at Reiko. Reiko took one step toward him and he shoved Bonnie aside and scrambled aboard the plane, almost taking the top of his head off on the door. This slight misjudgment made a noise like a crunching cantaloupe and was a very satisfying sound indeed.

Big John, another of Canada Goose Airways pilots, gave us a surreptitious OK sign and shoved the plane's nose toward deep water, and a few minutes later the whole area around Lost Lake was reverberating with the noise of his taking off. We were alone at last, and despite the fact that we were deep, deep in the bush and strictly dependent on each other (which was not too comforting), we felt for the first time that our new home was at last—home.

That evening, as we sat next to the big picture windows facing out over the lake, hoping we would see the northern lights or maybe a great horned owl, a loon laughed crazily, off in the descending dusk.

"Papa, where is my sled?" Bobby said.

"Your sled?" I asked. "It's only October. What do you want your sled for?"

"Because it's snowing." Bobby was right.

"Yeah," I said. "Snowing."

"What are we going to do?" Reiko said.

"About what?"

"The roof. It's snowing! The roof isn't finished!"

"What do you want me to do?" I said. "Get up there and finish it in a raging blizzard?"

"I won't need my sled now," Bobby said.

"Why not?" Reiko said.

"It stopped snowing."

"You see," I said, "always the big panic about everything. No wonder so many people get hurt during those Japanese earthquakes. You panic."

"Papa," Bobby said, "where's my sled?"

"How the hell do I—why?"

"It's snowing again." Reiko quietly crossed to the radiophone and called Kerry. At that time of night the other fourteen people we shared the radiophone channel with were either asleep or too exhausted to talk anymore that day, so she got the operator almost immediately.

"Sandy, this is Reiko Douglas. What happened?" What happened must have been plenty because Reiko didn't speak again for fifteen minutes; then she turned to me and said, "Clyde is a dirty double-crossing rat!"

"That's news?" I said.

Then Reiko turned back to the telephone. "Sandy, can you and Bill come back and work for us without Clyde?"

Bill and Sandy were back the next day. And from then on they worked like they were trying to finish the world by Sunday. I have never seen such energy and such dedication. Their coffee breaks lasted only five minutes, which was their idea, and the roof was completed in three days. So let it snow.

Our evenings were livened now by long talks of Bonnie and Clyde, as told by Sandy and Bill. It seems that in all the time we were absent from camp, Clyde and Bonnie spent most of the day in their cabin. Sandy and Bill, who had been told to wait for orders, did as much as they could with the project, then would have to wait until Clyde Rockcock crawled out from under the steamy Hudson Bay blanket and back to his administrative job. This had slowed everything up—including the coffee breaks, which we learned had only been restored for our benefit, as had the sumptuous dinners, lunches, and breakfasts we had seen served by the female James Beard while we were on hand. Before that, they had had beans and bread. Apparently all the good stuff had been reshipped to Kerry and the Bonnie's clan. The steaks, chops, turkeys, chickens, and other goodies had never been seen at Lost Lake.

Bonnie's mother, we learned, had been a frequent visitor, just to make sure her little girl was saying her daily prayers and wasn't getting too pregnant. Kerry's candidate for Mother of the Year made these chaperonic trips via Canada Goose Airways and charged them to me, which made me feel good all over.

Also, Clyde had told me, he and Bonnie were going to be married the first week in November, and he told Sandy and

Bill that I was going to send him and his lovely new bride to Acapulco for their honeymoon. All paid for with my Diners' Club card. As it turned out, Clyde kept postponing the wedding after he left my employ, presumably because he no longer urgently needed a backwoods cook and a handy penis holster. At this writing, Clyde is among the missing, at least in the town of Kerry, but Bonnie is back there with her mother, where she should be at a time like this.

One night after dinner, and just before the endless and inevitable hockey game on television, we all were sitting around the huge open fireplace, burning the last of our winter's supply of white birch. (Jake just hadn't got around to cutting any more, because he was too busy dreading the idea.)

"When's Dean Martin gonna be here?" said Sandy.

"Huh?" I said.

"Dean Martin," said Bill. "When is he coming?"

"That's a lotta people," said Sandy, "for Thanksgiving dinner—you'll have to get more'n one turkey."

I said, "Wait a minute—Dean Martin and a lotta people are coming here . . . for Thanksgiving . . . dinner?"

"That's what Clyde told us," said Sandy. "He said that's why we had to have the job done before that."

"I haven't seen Dean Martin for ten or twelve years," I said.

"I wonder if he's changed much," Bill said.

"How many people is he bringing?" I said.

"Fifteen."

Reiko started poking the fire, so the room was showered with sparks, which is apparently an old Japanese custom. She does this every twenty minutes all winter long.

"I like Dean Martin," said Bobby. "He's funny."

"You also like Jerry Lewis," I said, just so Sandy and Bill wouldn't get the idea that Bobby was too bright.

"Do you think they'll stay overnight?" said Reiko. "We only have sixteen blankets."

"That works out pretty good," said Bill. "You'll have one left over."

"Maybe Dean likes two blankets—that'll work out pretty good, too," said Sandy.

Suddenly we were all so involved in discussing this nutty pronouncement of Clyde's that Bill and Sandy forgot about the TV hockey game entirely, which to me was the perfect way to end a day.

Dean Martin didn't show up on Thanksgiving Day, but Mr. and Mrs. Trilby did.

20

MR. and Mrs. Trilby, who never went anywhere, according to local legend, made an exception in our case. Although they both were in their late seventies or early nineties—it depended on who was telling the story—they just *had* to Ski-doo the 60 or more miles from their little cabin at Starvation Lake to Lost Lake to get a good look at the odd-ball who kept timber wolves, a cougar, a Jesus-5, and a Japanese wife and who lived much farther back in the bush than they did. By choice.

We were startled, this particular frosty, clear morning, to see them roaring toward us from the north end of our snow-sheathed lake. We were startled because the shock waves set up by their Ski-doo assaulted our delicate eardrums, which had almost been returned to their original healthy virgin state by days and nights of blessed silence. The Ski-doo, like other snowmobiles, was not designed for sneaky approaches. If it has a muffler, it's a well-kept secret, and for snowmobile enthusiasts, the noise is the cherry on top of the sundae. More about these new iron dogs of the Arctic later. They *deserve* more because they freed more people in the North than Lincoln did in the South.

Mr. and Mrs. Trilby circled our little island three times at high speed with a rooster tail of frozen snow arching into the crisp air; then, after this precaution, the Ski-doo slammed to an abrupt stop at the airplane dock, and two frost-rimed apparitions freed themselves from their icy seats with a definite peeling sound.

"We're Mr. and Mrs. Trilby," the first apparition said, in a voice which sounded like a child's first record player. "I'm Lambert Trilby and this"—indicating the other apparition, who was now lighting the last two inches of a wet cigar—"is my wife, Sandra."

"Goddamn Ski-doo," Sandra Trilby said, "we gotta get a bigger windshield, lamb, my goddamn cigar is stinking wet."

"Maybe on your birthday," Lambert Trilby said.

Lambert and Sandra Trilby were originals. Sandra Trilby, who was dressed in heavy pants and a quilted parka, wore a Jean Harlow blond wig over a face which was reptilian. I'm a little weak on my anthropology, but she definitely had turtle blood. Lambert Trilby looked exactly like his wife. I was nonplussed. How do you talk to turtles?

The jungle telegraph of the northern bush country hadn't been too accurate in their estimate of the Trilbys' age. They didn't look *seventy* or *eighty* or *ninety*. They looked like they had been found deep in the permafrost of the northern Siberian plains, close by a hairy mammoth graveyard, and revived by some mad doctor, with the aid of special vitamins and a lightning bolt. They were the oldest living humans—if they were really human and living.

Mr. and Mrs. Trilby were not too impressed by my wolves or the cougar, even when I demonstrated how friendly I had made them. After dutifully licking my face, the wolves gathered together in one corner of their run and stared, warily, at Mr. and Mrs. Trilby with unblinking amber eyes. The cougar climbed the wire siding of her pen and spat viciously. Mrs. Trilby seemed about to spit back, but changed her mind and said, "Pretty big cat—you must have a lot of mice."

"Not anymore," I said.

If our animals failed to make a dent in the Trilby's indifference, Reiko's appearance instantly changed everything. When she came out of our cabin in her pink ski pants and her fur parka, Mrs. Trilby's snapping lower jaw dropped open to her chest. "It's a doll!" she said. "A little live doll!" And that's the way Reiko looked as she walked toward us through the snow, the sun now brilliantly sparkling everything into diamonds. She did look like a little live doll as she smiled, the fur framing her lovely face, and her large dark-brown eyes, which looked deep into your soul, turning soft with the warm glow of welcome for these odd strangers.

Reiko *was* happy to see Lambert and Sandra Trilby. She didn't care if they were ancient and chimerical. They were *here!* No matter how she coveted it, I felt that Reiko had reached the point where she would have been happy to see the Boston Strangler—or Joe Bananas.

Urged, I'm sure, by the desire to please this Japanese toy, Lambert Trilby felt, as so many another amateur raconteur had before him, that a merry quip would get things started on the right foot, so he said to Reiko, "Do you like jokes?"

"Jack writes jokes," Reiko said. "He wrote jokes about Old New Litchridge—that's where we used to live—that's why we live up here now."

"You're not Catholic, are you?" Lambert said.

"What's *that?*" Reiko said.

"She's a Buddhist," I said.

"Good," Lambert said, stamping some warmth back into his snowmobile boots. "I got a joke about the Pope."

"Jack doesn't write jokes about the Pope," Reiko said.

"I'm freezin' my butt off standing out here," Sandra Trilby said.

"You know what the Pope said to the pregnant unmarried Irish girl?"

"Jack's father was Irish," Reiko said.

"I'm freezin' my butt off standing out here," Bobby said.

"The kid's right," Sandra said.

"Let's go inside," I said.

"Wait a minute!" Lambert bellowed. "I'll have to start *all over again!* Now *what* in *hell* did the *Pope* say to the *crazy knocked-up unmarried Irish girl?*"

"For *crissakes, what?*" Sandra shouted back.

The wolves started to howl and the cougar started tearing around her cage in a demented dash to nowhere.

"Keep the baby, Faith!" Lambert screamed above what was now double pandemonium. With this, all sound suddenly ceased, and Lambert just stood there, stunned.

"Don'tcha get it?" he whispered, pleadingly. Turning from

one to another. His eyes begging for a tiny scrap of appreciation.

When he got to Bobby, Bobby said, "I'm freezin' my butt off standing here."

"Would you like-a tea?" Reiko said.

"I would," Sandra Trilby said, "with a large spot of brandy in it."

"Follow me," Reiko said, and we left the wary wolves and the spitting cougar to their own devices, which suited them fine, and trooped into the house.

Sitting as close as possible to our nonheating fireplace and sipping our tea, I asked Lambert how they kept busy back in the bush. I was sure these two museum pieces didn't sit around all day twiddling their gray thumbs. They had too much energy and bounce.

Before Lambert could answer, Reiko asked, "Have you folks lived up here in the woods all your lives?"

"Hell, no," Sandra said. "We come here right after we quit show business," Sandra said, sipping her brandy with a spot of tea in it.

"Show business!" I couldn't believe it.

"Sure," Lambert said. "Vaudeville. We used to be a comedy team—Trilby and Trilby?" He waited for some sign of recognition this grand old show business name should have generated, but contrary to my usual behavior under such circumstances, this time I could not force myself to say, "Oh, yes—I remember—very well." The whole idea was too bizarre. If the Trilbys were in vaudeville, it must have been around the turn of the century. And probably not *this* century.

"Lambert used to be a comic," Sandra said. "Oh, he was *funny,* always telling jokes—on or off—it didn't matter to him. Tell them the joke about the Pope and the pregnant Irish girl—"

"Well," said Lambert, "there was this Pope, see—and he was talkin' to this pregnant Irish girl—"

"She wasn't married," Sandra said. "That's the *best* part."

"Oh, yeah," Lambert said. "This pregnant Irish girl—"

"Oh, *this* is *funny!*" Sandra said, and immediately shrieked herself into a fit of hysterical laughter which segued into a choking fit.

"She's the greatest audience in the world," Lambert said.

"I better get her a glass of water," I said.

"Don't bother," Lambert said. "After she faints, she'll snap out of it."

Reiko tried to help as Sandra fainted and slithered untidily to the floor, her complexion turning from a weathered gray to a mauve green. Lambert added, "Don't worry about Sandra-baby. She's got everything going for her—she's a Christian Scientist and she's got Blue Cross."

As Sandra-baby lay on the floor, Lambert nudged her gently with the toe of his boot and said, "Wonderful little lady—washes all her colored things in lime Koolaid."

"What the *hell* does *that* mean?" I said.

Lambert didn't bother to answer, and when Sandra-baby fluttered open her lashless lids, she looked around the room and said, "Bad trip."

"Would you like-a tea?" Reiko said.

"It's a doll!" Sandra said. "A little live doll!"

I wanted to know more about how the Trilbys lived—at their age—far from any of the so-called creature comforts of civilization.

"We trap a little," Lambert said.

"A little what?" Reiko wanted to know.

"Beavers mostly," Lambert said.

"We got a beaver," Bobby said. "He's a *big* sonofabitch!"

"Bobby!" Reiko said. "You're not supposed to say that. Only in the family. And we don't have a beaver. That beaver we see belongs to the lake."

"He's a *big* sonofabitch!" Bobby, naturally, repeated.

We invited Mr. and Mrs. Trilby to stay for Thanksgiving dinner. They accepted, but they were puzzled. "Thanksgiving Day was last month," Sandra said, lighting another two-inch wet cigar and taking the first ballet position against the bar, hoping, I presume, that Edgar Degas might drop in and immortalize her on canvas for the hotel owners of America.

"Yeah," Lambert said, "in Canada we celebrate Thanksgiving on the second Monday of October. Why do you Yanks celebrate it in November?" I explained that it was an old Pilgrim tradition. These first poor souls to arrive in the land of the free were so grateful that they had survived a New England winter they wanted to thank God.

Lambert laughed a little and said, "We Canadians thank God because the first settlers were glad to be alive after May and June." I thought he was putting me on, but he continued to say that from May 15 to June 7 is the blackfly season. "Millions of these little black sonsabitches," he said.

"Please, Lambert," Sandra said, "only in the family!"

"I'm sorry, Mrs. Douglas," Lambert said, turning to Reiko, who wasn't listening, "but you wait. You'll see what I mean— it's the *only* way you can describe them." Reiko was listening now.

"Er, Mr. Trilby," I said, quickly trying to steer the conversation away from any more problems to be added to our already jam-packed problem calendar, "what's it like to live in the bush?"

"Well," said Lambert, "it ain't no Miami Beach."

"Would you rather live—in Miami Beach?" I said, with a feeling that my safe little rug was slowly being inched out from under me. I loved this country and I wanted everyone else to feel the same way—even those who had spent most of their lives among the murmuring pines and hemlocks, where the deer and the antelope are being conscientiously depleted.

"Hell, no!" I was relieved to hear Lambert and Sandra both say. "They ain't even got a beach in Miami Beach!" Lambert said.

"Oh, they got a beach all right," Sandra said, "but it's only three inches wide."

"She's right, *by gar!* That's what the French Canadians say," he interrupted. "You know all them photos you see— girls runnin' up and down the beach in bikinis playing volleyball or whatever—you know where they take them photos! *Waikiki—Hawaii!*"

"I doubt that," I said. "The beach at Waikiki is only *two* inches wide—at low tide."

This brought Lambert up short. I had snatched away his favorite dream. I felt like a rat.

"How about Long Beach, California?" Lambert was growing desperate.

"No," I said, "they used to have a magnificent beach there, but they laid the *Queen Mary* on it and covered the whole thing up. When they bought it, they didn't figure on its being so big."

"Didn't they measure it before they bought it?" Sandra said.

"No," I said. "That's the way they do things in California.

They grab something big, lay it on the beach; then they measure it afterward."

"Are we still talkin' about the *Queen Mary?*" Lambert said.

"Why don't you go to Tahiti?" Reiko shouted from the kitchen, where she was soy saucing the Thanksgiving turkey. "They've got plenty of beaches there—with black sand!"

"Black sand!" the Trilbys chorused.

"Yes," I said, "it comes from volcanoes."

"I know what a volcano is," Bobby said.

"Sure you do," I said. "It's a big sonofabitch—right?"

"Gee, Papa," Bobby said, "how did you know?"

"Bobby," I said, "why don't you go fish through the ice?"

"I don't got no worms," Bobby said, skillfully using the faultless grammar he had learned at the Happy Child Nursery School back in Old New Litchridge.

"Nobody don't got no worms at this time a year," Lambert said.

"Did you go to the Happy Child Nursery School?" asked Reiko. "I mean, when you were a child?"

"I don't remember," Lambert said.

"Do you know Jake Moon?" I asked. "He works for us."

"Good man."

"You know him?" asked Reiko.

"No," Lambert said, "but that's what we always say up here—'Good man.'"

"He's a sonofabitch!" Bobby said.

"Bobby!" I said.

"That's what you always call him, Papa," Bobby said; then he started to cry—afraid that he had committed an error. Little did the poor kid know that he was batting a thousand.

"This Jake Moon," I explained to the Trilbys, "is something less than perfect."

"Hard to get help in the bush these days," Sandra said.

"Yeah," Lambert said, "and nowadays they want carfare, too."

"We used to have Indians back in the old days. We used to pay 'em off with whiskey," Sandra said.

"I thought that was illegal," I said.

"Yeah," Lambert said, "but it sure got the dishes done in a hurry."

"Where's this Jake Moon today?" Lambert asked. "Is he working?"

"No," I said. "He had to go to a funeral."

"Whose funeral?"

"Somebody named Morton," Reiko said.

"Yeah," I said. "Haynes Morton. That's whose."

"Haynes Morton!" Lambert said, his squinty eyes wide. "He died three years ago!"

"Gee," Reiko said, "what'll Jake do when he gets to town and finds out he's three years late for Mr. Morton's funeral?"

"Maybe he'll commit suicide so he can go to *somebody's* funeral."

"What's that mean?" Reiko said.

"Good man, that Jake Moon," Lambert said.

"Amen," Sandra said.

"Shit," Bobby said.

"Only in the *family!*" Reiko said.

21

THE moose-hunting season is mercifully short in the North Chinook Bay Wilderness Reserve, in which we live. Anyone who has seen one of these magnificent animals, who have the distinction of being the largest, most powerful deer in the world, standing belly-deep in a swampy north country pond or slipping through the brush without cracking a twig must admit that it is one of nature's most awesome sights. A moose is not pretty, but its size and bearing make it a regal creature indeed. A regal creature which may be brought floundering helplessly to its knees by a bullet from the rifle of nature's puniest predator.

We not only were concerned for the moose we had seen

quite often near our camp and which we liked to think were the same ones each time and which we had given names like Frankie Big Nose and Emily Little Feet, but also for Tanuki and our other wolves, plus Pussycat and the dogs. There had been a bloody incident a couple of years previously, where some overeager "sportsman" had shot and killed six sled dogs, whom their owner had tied for the night to six small trees in an open clearing. This wanton mistake was explained. "I thought they were wolves," the butcher said.

During the hunting season, my rifle is never too far from me, and if any hunters approach our animal corrals or draw a bead on Doggie or Chibi, it will be their last earthly act— and I have the perfect alibi. I'll just say, "I thought they were people."

The moose-hunting season was in full swing during our first November in the bush, and although we had seen no hunters, we had heard an occasional rifleshot, which made us sad, but there was nothing we could do—except pray for the moose. As the crisp, cold, and exceptionally clear days went by, the sound of shots grew fewer, and by the last day of the hunting season we heard nothing but the soft crinkle-tinkle of millions of bells as the ice started forming on the lake. I think we were happier than the moose that the unfair contest was over until next year.

At three o'clock in the afternoon of that last day, we were suddenly astounded by the flying figure of what looked like an Indian, in full chief's regalia, running madly up the path toward the lodge.

"What's that?" Reiko said.

"That's Pocahontas," Bobby said, remembering some of the history lesson I had just finished giving him.

"Pocahontas was a girl," I said.

"*That's* not a girl," Reiko said, peeking through the curtains, "but she is running like a girl."

"What's she running for?" Bobby said. "I don't see any bears. Maybe she has to go to the bathroom."

"Not *our* bathroom," Reiko said. "Our bathroom is only for the family."

By this time the Indian had climbed the steep path up to the lodge and started to pound on the door. "Let me in!" he said. "Please, let me in!" He sounded hysterical. I let him in.

"You wanna use the bathroom?" Bobby said.

"Not anymore," the Indian said, gasping for breath.

"What happened?" I said, leading him to a couch and help-ing him with his rifle and his buckskin hunting bag. He threw himself down, bending the feathers he had stuck in his wool stocking cap.

"Are you an Indian?" Bobby asked.

"Of course I'm an Indian," the Indian said, with a decided lisp and a slight pout. "Whaddya think this is"—indicating his red-brown face—"makeup!"

"It's very streaky-looking," Reiko said. "Have you been crying?"

Instantly the Indian was on his feet in front of the bar mirror. "Oh!" he said. "I'm a mess. Look at that hair! No body to it at *all!* That lousy spray for brunettes only doesn't mean a goddamn thing!"

This whole thing was beginning to take on *Twilight Zone* feeling. I was sure it was some kind of a put-on, but why?

"Look," I said. "I don't mean to presume on your private life, but we're a little puzzled. What are you doing running through the bush dressed up like an Indian?"

"Because I *am* an Indian," he said, with a dainty stomp of his beaded moccasined foot.

"You look Jewish," Reiko said, with her usual honesty.

"*All* Indians look Jewish!" the Indian said, the pitch of his voice changing from low to mezzo-soprano.

"All Jewish don't look like Indians," Reiko persisted.

"Listen!" said the Indian, somewhat waspishly, the large brass pendant hanging from his love beads clanging against the silver buttons of his lavender buckskin shirt. "No matter *what* you think—I'm an *Indian!*"

"What's your name," Bobby said, "Chief Running Deer?"

"No," the Indian said.

"Chief Red Cloud?" Bobby said.

"No."

"Chief *White* Cloud?"

"No."

Bobby was stuck for a moment; then he said, "Blue Cloud?"

I felt that Bobby had exhausted colors, so I said, "Then what *is* your name?"

"You'll only laugh," the Indian said.

"No, I won't," I said.

"Sure?"

"Yes, I'm sure."

"It's Stanley Shapiro."

I laughed.

"I can *explain!*" the poor Indian screamed. "I was captured by a Jewish family when I was two years old, and I adopted their tribal name!"

"Oh, come on!" I said.

"Lousy story, isn't it?" the Indian said.

"It needs work," I said. "Now tell us—what the hell are you doing all by yourself way up here in the bush?"

"I'm a guide. An *Indian* guide. It sounds better to the tourists," he said. "I was guiding a party of moose hunters, and they got mad at me, so I ran away and left them. I hope they get lost and *nobody* ever finds them! Oh—they were such boors! So gauche! So *insistent!*"

"Insistent? On what?"

"Insistent I find them a moose! How could *I* find them a moose? This is my first time as a guide. An *Indian* guide! They just didn't understand. There's no place for a new Indian guide to *practice!* They didn't give me a chance! They weren't patient at *all!*"

"Hunters very seldom are," I said.

"Oh, I could just *cry* when I think of how much money I spent learning to be an Indian guide. And it's *nothing* like they said it would be! I thought all I would have to do is walk through the woods and point the way, but it didn't turn out like that at *all!* I had to build a *fire* and *cook* and carry a *canoe* on my *head.*"

"You shouldn't carry a canoe on your head when you're cooking," Reiko said, and I believed her, because there was nothing she didn't know about cooking.

I was still sure that one of my show biz friends had sent this character up here as some sort of weird practical joke, but how he managed to get where we are was a mystery. It was quite cold and snowy and too far to walk, and we had heard no plane landing nearby. Or the noise of a snowmobile.

"You look Jewish," Reiko repeated.

"That's because I *am* Jewish," he said, quite impatiently now. "How else could I pass as an *Indian?* There are some things you just can't *fake!*"

"Who sent you?" I said. "Abe Burrows? Mel Brooks? Gene Saks? Pearl Bailey?"

"Who?" he said.

"Another Indian," I said. "Now come on—who sent you up here to pull a practical joke on me?"

"Gene Saks is a nice man," Reiko said. "He was going to direct one of my husband's plays, but the play was a big flop in Westport, Connecticut. Jack-san hasn't written a big flop play since."

"I haven't *tried*," I said, cut to the quick.

"I was in a play at the Westport Playhouse," the Indian said. "I played the part of an Indian—that's how I got the idea to be an Indian guide in Canada. I didn't make good as an Indian in Westport."

"Were you in Jack-san's play?" Reiko said.

"Now wait a minute," I said, "this whole thing is getting out of control. I want to know who sent you up here to us."

"My right hand to God," the Indian said, "nobody sent me. And I never even knew you were here. My name is Stanley Shapiro, and I saw this article in the *Village Voice* about how gay it was being an Indian guide, and I was fed up with Eighth Street and Washington Square and Macdougal Alley and little thin pancakes, and fat, smelly, secondhand maggoty people with moldy beards—and the men are even worse." There wasn't a trace of a smile on his face, so I accepted this last.

"You're not just dodging the draft?" I said.

"Who'd take me?" he said. "I couldn't even get in the Liechtenstein Brownies—if they waived the physical."

"*Are* you dodging the draft?" Reiko insisted.

"Well, yes," Stanley said, "but *only* for the *duration*. I thought I could come up here and start a new life, but so far I don't know—I *just don't know!*"

"Maybe the Army would be easier," I said.

"But I *love* it up *here*—I *really love* it—but they don't love me. Right now, that Mr. Virgil Clarke and Mr. Harry Cougle and that Mr. Peter Sprole are out looking for me. They wanted to shoot a moose, but all I ever guided them to was a couple of rabbits and a dead owl, who had bumped into a duck in the dark. Those fellows are furious! You must help me!" As Stanley Shapiro was confessing, I couldn't help wondering how he, even in his wildest imagination, could hope to pass himself off as an Indian guide. Even with his aboriginal trappings, he looked more like Tiny Tim than Sitting Bull. There must be a terrific shortage of guides—plus a black market in guide licenses—or he never would have made it past the Sheep Meadow in New York's Central Park.

"Papa," Bobby said, "some men are coming."

"My God," Stanley Shapiro squealed, "it's them, Mr. Clarke, Mr. Cougle and Mr. Sprole—they'll kill me."

"I don't think so," I said. "The season for Shapiros doesn't open until next month."

Stanley looked at me, his eyes wide and his mouth open.

"Yeah," Bobby said, "next month."

"What are *you* talking about?" I said to Bobby.

"Nothing," Bobby said, "but children are supposed to be included in the conversation—that's what Dr. Ginott says."

"Oh?" I said. "And where did you hear Dr. Ginott say this?"

"On television," Bobby said, "on the 'And *here's* Johnny!' show."

"What did Johnny say about children?" Reiko said.

"Nothing," Bobby said. "It was time for a commercial."

"Is this going to be a long discussion?" Stanley quivered. "Because if it is, I'm going to hide somewhere because those savages are coming closer and closer and," he added, peering anxiously with one eye from behind the curtains, "they look pretty mad."

"Go hide in the bathroom," I said.

"No," Stanley said, "suppose one of them wants to use it?"

"Not my bathroom!" Reiko said. "That's for the family. Not for moose shooters."

We got Stanley safely up into a small loft, off the kitchen, where he couldn't be seen, just as the three "moose shooters" arrived at the front door. They knocked a bit too authoritatively, I thought, and immediately my small supply of warm hospitality cooled to the vanishing point. I hid the scotch before I opened the front door.

"I'm Virge Clarke, and this is Harry Cougle, and this old reprobate (ha-ha) is Pete Sprole."

"Would you like-a tea?" Reiko said.

All three of them glanced at our fancy frontier bar and reluctantly agreed that they thought tea would be charming.

As soon as Reiko had taken off for the kitchen, Virge said,

"You didn't see a dirty bastard of an Indian guide around here, did you?"

"I saw a moose," Bobby said.

"Where? Where? Where?" they all said, grabbing their rifles, viciously elbowing one another out of the way toward the door.

"Right out in back of Papa's office," Bobby said, pointing in that direction. Bobby's timing was perfect—he waited until the third "moose shooter" had flung himself through the doorway before he said, "Last summer."

The three returned surlily, looking at Bobby with ill-disguised glances of surprised distrust.

"I saw a moose about fifteen minutes ago over on that point," I said, indicating a small peninsula not more than a hundred yards from the house. They all jumped up again, then wearily changed their minds.

"To hell with it," Virge said. "I couldn't walk that far. That sonofabitchin' Indian had us all over this whole sonofa-bitchin' country, and we didn't see one sonofabitchin' moose."

"We didn't even see any sonofabitchin' moose sonofabitchin' shit," Pete said.

"Funny," I said. "Sonofabitchin' funny."

"Yeah," Virge said. "What am I gonna tell the little woman? I promised her a moose."

"Why don't you give her a nice bunny rabbit?" Reiko said, bringing in the tea. "Bunny rabbits are much easier to take care of. You don't need much room and a little lettuce and a few carrots and that's about all there is to it."

I had never heard such a long sentence from Reiko since we were married. I'm sure she had been rehearsing in the kitchen, waiting for the water to boil.

The "moose shooters" had nothing to say about this gentle suggestion; they just sat drinking their nice cup of tea and looking longingly at the bar. But I was adamant—no booze for butchers.

"I don't think that Indian knew what he was doin' at all," Virge said.

"Where did you get him?" I said.

"He stopped Pete in the street and asked him if he wanted a guide. He said he knew where there was plenty of moose."

"I don't even think he was an Indian," Pete said.

"Why?" I asked.

"Because he used the same kinda perfume as my wife does—My Sin. Who ever heard of an Indian using My Sin?"

"I think he was a faggot," Harry said, between unsatisfying sips of tea.

"What's a faggot?" Bobby promptly asked.

"Like a fairy," I said. "You know—like the tooth fairy."

"Oh," Bobby said, "I got an idea. From now on, I'm gonna call him the tooth faggot."

"Good," I said.

"What's a tooth faggot?" Reiko said, forcing more tea on the "moose shooters."

"It's a faggot with teeth," I said.

"You know what we call faggots in Japan?" Reiko said.

"No. What?"

"Homosexuals."

"What's a homo—" Bobby started.

"Bobby," I said, "go for a swim."

"Papa, it's snowing!" he said.

"Then put on your warm swimsuit," I said.

"Papa's funny," Bobby informed the sour "moose shooters."

"Yeah," said Virge. Pete and Harry just ground their teeth.

"Well," I said, when I saw that there was little chance for the gloom to lift, "gotta get busy. Reiko's gotta get dinner ready and I have to bring in some firewood for the fireplace. Looks like it's going to be a cold one tonight. Where are you staying?"

"We're campin'—in a *tent*," Virge said. "Over at Loon Lake."

"That's a long way from here," Bobby said helpfully.

The three "moose shooters" stood up, took one last look at the bar, and crawled toward the front door. Virge started to talk, "If you ever see that—that Indian—"

"I'll tell him he's a sonofabitch—right?"

Virge just looked at me, then followed Pete and Harry down the path and toward Loon Lake. They saw Tanuki and the other wolves and the cougar, but their spirit of the hunt had dulled to a point of utter indifference. I had a feeling if they saw a moose now, they would just wave a forlorn hello and keep right on walking the long trail back to their camp.

We kept Stanley Shapiro for a few days, hoping that he might work out as a replacement for Jake, but even though he begged to remain—"I'll cook for you. I'll sew for you. I'll chop wood for you. I'll get the mail for you! I'll feed the bears for you. I'll make the beds and clean your oven for you"—we decided that although it would have been nice to have a draft dodger Indian guide around as a conversation piece, he ate more than all the animals together, and he never stopped talking. Also, his actual knowledge of the rugged Canadian bush country was on a par with Lee Radziwill's. So we snowmobiled him to the highway, where his leave-taking was so extravagantly dramatic, I felt we were taking part in an Isadora Duncan revival.

The last I heard of Stanley Shapiro he was back in New York, still dodging the draft, had changed his name to Genghis Khan, and was guiding tourist buses through Chinatown.

22

WHEN we first arrived at Lost Lake, I had Bobby's educational program all arranged. Or I should say, I had arranged mentally the routine which would have to be followed to get him to the General Montcalm Primary School, which was approximately 100 miles, as the school bus flies, from our woodland glen. Mentally everything worked out just fine.

In practice it worked out just like Waterloo for that short little man with the cold hand. Everything had to be timed to the minute. We had to get up at 5:40 A.M. to leave the boat dock at 6:40 in order to sail across the lake, drive down the timber road, and meet the school bus at 7:40 at Highway 365. Then I would drive back over the ghastly timber road to the boat, sail across the lake, and crawl into my office to work. At 3:30 P.M. I reversed the process to meet the school bus on Highway 365 at 4:30, then back down the timber road as darkness set in, which gave the whole thing a sense of adventure for the first few trips, but after that, Bobby and I stopped the fun game of seeing the shadowy forms of hostile Indians and giant bears and other assorted divertissement and settled down to an endless silent journey. Sometimes we didn't know whether we were going or on our way back. Bobby didn't actually start at the General Montcalm Primary School till November, months after we had emigrated to the land of the sky blue water, so it wasn't too long before both the morning and the afternoon journeys were made in the dark. And the sky blue water was pitch black.

Bobby didn't seem to mind the long bus trip, but I was rapidly coming to the conclusion that a formal education wasn't everything. And it wasn't too long before I decided that it was a distinct handicap. After all, there were many millionaires in the world who hadn't gone beyond the third grade. Lincoln used to write all his stuff on the back of a shovel with a piece of charcoal. He wasn't a millionaire, but his face is a couple of hundred feet high at Mount Rushmore.

Along about the second week of dashing through the woods at dawn, I told this to Reiko. I said, "Lincoln used to write on the back of a shovel—at home!"

"I don't want a shovel inside the house," Reiko said, "and I don't want Bobby to be the President. I want him to be a lawyer."

"Lincoln *was* a lawyer," I said.

"I thought he was the President," she said.

"He was, but he was a lawyer first. Later he switched to being President."

"No wonder," Reiko said. "Who'd want a lawyer who wrote on the back of shovels!" I thought this was the Japanese version of a leg-pulling but it wasn't—this was Japanese logic, which was at times on a par with Tarzan's oversimplified "Me Tarzan—You Jane," which now, at any gay bar, has become "Me Tarzan—You Tarzan." Which cuts through a lot of red tape.

One very cool November morning the Land Rover got stuck in the quicksand causeway crossing the swamp, and Bobby and I had a choice: Either we could walk to the school bus, which was about five miles, or we could walk back to the north end of Lost Lake, which was about five miles. The swamp was the halfway mark between nowhere and nowhere else. We decided very quickly that it would be better to return to Lost Lake and call for help—what kind of help I hadn't figured out, because no tow truck could have traversed that timber road without having to call on another tow truck for assistance.

I hadn't walked five miles in years, but I thought we could make it, and also we might see a few animals, which we wouldn't have, driving a noisy Land Rover. We had sandwiches and my emergency Cokes—even a spare set of snowshoes—so we weren't in too much trouble. I don't know what it is about me and Coca-Cola—I treat a bottle of Coke like it was plasma or the cure for terminal heartburn. I felt *safe* with a bottle of Coke, and it looked better than sucking my thumb at civil defense meetings.

Trudging down the long miles of the timber road, Bobby felt safe with me, because I was his Papa, but if ever there was a misguided trust in the invincibility of a father, this was it. In case of a real forest emergency I wouldn't have had the foggiest of what to do. The basics I knew—if you wanted to take a leak in the woods, you go behind a tree. If you wanted to start a fire, you rubbed something together, and if you wanted shelter, you found a cave—preferably unoccupied. How to snare a moose with the unravelings of my wool socks, in case we got hungry, I really hadn't practiced much. But I wished I had, after the sandwiches had been consumed. After an hour or so we got hungry. Very hungry.

"Why don't we do like Charlie Chaplin?" Bobby said.

"What do you mean?" I said.

"Don't you remember that movie, Papa? Charlie Chaplin got so hungry he ate his shoes. We got some extra snowshoes."

"Oh, yes," I said. "But if we eat our snowshoes, maybe it will spoil our dinner and Mommy will get mad."

After walking another long hour or so, Bobby stopped and said, "I think I'm gonna spoil my dinner."

The snowshoes were beginning to look delicious, when I noticed we were close to a tall tamarack tree which had been stripped naked on one side by lightning. This tree was only a mile from the north end of Lost Lake, so I prevailed on Bobby to give up his trailside snack and slog onward.

When we arrived at the lake and lay gasping in the grass,

Bobby said, "Papa, let's buy a nice big shovel and a nice big bag of charcoal."

So that's how it happened. That's how I became a first-grade teacher in a one-room schoolhouse with one pupil. We didn't use shovel and charcoal. We used something called "Miss Pickersgill's First Grade Home Study Course." I don't know whether there actually was a Miss Pickersgill, but there sure was a home study course (insisted upon by the Canadian government for bush children), which arrived by mail via Canada Goose Airways once every two weeks.

I felt that in order to make this weird operation work successfully, I would have to conduct it as much as possible like a real school. Promptly each morning I rang a very large ship's bell, which once was part of life at Lost Lake, when they used to have huge groups of business tycoons up here for booze and fishing. This bell, which could be heard for miles, had summoned the guests back to the main lodge. It now summoned Bobby to school—very reluctantly.

School was held in my cabin office, which was some distance from where he lived, so in one way, it created the illusion that he was leaving home for the day and going to school.

When Bobby arrived gloomily at school I made him take off his boots and his fur parka and sit at a school desk, which was a piece of plywood held up by two sawhorses. Then I'd call the roll. This was necessarily a very short ceremony— until he decided to take the Fifth Amendment and not answer at all. After roll call we stood and repeated the pledge of allegiance to the flag. The American flag. But of course, living in Canada, after the pledge of allegiance to the Stars and Stripes and the singing of "America," we face the other side of the little room and pledge, not allegiance, but to be good residents of Canada, and sing "God Save the Queen" and maybe a couple of songs from *Oliver*. If everything is holding up well, we light a candle in front of a small plaster statue of St. Gerbil, who has replaced Danny Kaye as the patron saint of children. After this, the school day starts.

The new math I ignore completely because Miss Pickersgill seems a bit confused herself about this. Spelling, reading, and writing don't seem too difficult for either of us. I mean Bobby and me. His writing is better than mine because I studied under the New York State school system, long before the teachers were organized, so there were no strikes and the teachers were always present, which made it difficult to really settle down and learn anything. I didn't find out about how to picket or protest until I was nearly twenty-five years old. By that time my old school had burned down and all we had left to protest and picket was a big hole in the ground. This was a stickler, but some who were smarter than the rest of us thought of a reason to picket a big hole in the ground. Our picket signs read: THIS SWIMMING POOL HAS NEVER BEEN COMPLETED BECAUSE OF DOW CHEMICAL! And others carried signs reading MAKE WAVES—NOT WAR! One skinny pimply-faced lad carried a sign which read BRING OUR GIRLS BACK! I said to him, "What girls?" and he said, "Who cares! I gotta get rid of these pimples."

But to return to the little red schoolhouse in the pines. After an hour or two of tearful teachings, I rang a bell which meant recess.

"What are you ringing the bell for, Papa?" Bobby said.

"Recess," I said. "Now you can go outside and play with all your little friends."

"Whaddya mean," Bobby said, "go outside and play with all my little friends? *What* little friends?"

"Go find a frog," I said, "and be nice to him—maybe he'll become your friend."

"Papa," Bobby said, "that's crazy."

"No, it isn't," I said. "Ask the frog if he knows any other nice frogs; then you'll have lots of friends."

Bobby decided that even though I was his Papa, I didn't have all my marbles, which was true, but desperate times called for desperate measures. The Birdman of Alcatraz didn't have any friends, so he cozied up to some sparrows, and pretty soon he had enough sparrow friends to tie together and fly him off the island.

Recess was never much of a success. I finally had to go outside with Bobby and we played touch football and hide-and-seek. Hide-and-seek was only played once because in the thousands of square miles of places to hide which surrounded us, seeking could take all the recess period and the rest of the week. I thought Bobby had become a first-grade dropout after our first game.

The home-teaching school was not exactly a success, nor was it a failure. Miss Pickersgill, who seemed to be rather absent-minded, once in a while sent us the lessons printed in the Eskimo or Aleut language, which I thought was the new math, until Charlie Burke, who had flown all over Canada, explained. Charlie could speak some Eskimo and Aleut, which was fascinating to listen to if you were an Eskimo or an Aleut or stoned. Or all three. Then it was better than LSD.

I don't really know yet whether Bobby was helped or hindered by my teaching, but I do know that I got goddamn sick and tired of " 'Run, Mary, run,' said Mike."

" 'I am running,' said Mary."

" 'Run harder,' said Mike."

" 'I am running harder,' said Mary."

" 'The cow will catch us if you don't run harder,' said Mike."

" 'What cow?' said Mary."

Or

" 'I want to go to the moon,' said Jeff."

" 'How can you go to the moon?' said Mary. 'You don't have a rocket.' "

" 'I will make a rocket,' said Jeff."

" 'How?' said Cappy [whoever *he* is]."

" 'I will make a rocket out of this cornflakes box,' said Jeff."

" 'You're fulla crap and you're drunk!' said Mary." This last wasn't in the *Golden Book of Boring Stories,* but it should have been. That's the way Jeff and Mary *really* talk.

The school year back in the bush had more holidays than any other school in the world. I had to resort to the *World Almanac,* the *Encyclopaedia Britannica,* and a little-known volume called *Little-Known Holidays.* We celebrated every holiday from Purim to the St. Bartholomew's Day Massacre —which was a holiday, we reasoned, for them that got massacred, anyway.

Holidays and recess (which got longer and longer during the school year) was the only way we survived the first grade. But Miss Pickersgill was very pleased because even though Bobby flunked, *I* passed.

This home school idea hung like a pall over our summer

vacation because the second grade was staring us in the face
and grinning like the most unpleasant one of the Four
Horsemen. I knew that neither one of us would come
through it alive. Just before the fall term I switched Bobby
from Miss Pickersgill to the Talmadge School of Applied
Taxidermy.

23

MR. and Mrs. Trilby, the ancient odd couple who were our
nearest neighbors, won $500 in a soap contest, or rather, Mr.
Trilby hád. Charlie Burke flew them into Lost Lake for their
first airplane trip—prompted by this unexpected windfall.
This was more actual cash than they'd ever had in their
whole life and they wanted to "go somewhere," so they came
to visit us, because they adored Reiko.

"It was easy," Lambert Trilby said, with the quiet confidence of someone who has it made. "All I had to do was
finish the sentence 'I like Simpkins Soap because—in twenty-
five words or less,' so I said, 'I like Simpkins Soap because
I'm dirty.'"

"Is it a good soap?" Reiko asked.

"I dunno," Lambert said. "We never used it. We make our
own soap."

"Yeah," Sandra Trilby said, "we make it outta beaver fat
and lye—you want the recipe?"

"I do," Charlie Burke said.

"Oh, you do, huh?" I said. "Why?"

"You never can tell," Charlie said, "next week they may
have a contest—'I like beaver fat and lye.'"

"I think you'll need more than twenty-five words to explain
that," I said.

"Would you like-a tea?" Reiko said. (Whenever Caucasian conversation got too much for her, this was her only defense—"Would you like-a tea?")

"Charlie," I said, "aren't you supposed to be due back at the base? Isn't this the moose-hunting season?"

"Yeah," Charlie said, but he made no move to go. Canada Goose Airways flew hunters back into the bush during the moose season, but Charlie didn't approve of these "sportsmen," and when a moose was spotted from the air, and the hunters, who had usually drunk their breakfast, frantically urged him to land immediately, Charlie would say, "Yes, sir," and circle just long enough, before he landed, to confuse the hunters completely. Then, after easing the plane to shore, he would point in the opposite direction from where the moose was peacefully filling its belly with cedar boughs and say, "He's right over that little rise. Good luck. I'll be back for you later." The hunters would stumble and stagger off in wild anticipation; then Charlie would fly back to where the moose was grazing and dip his wings. The moose would just go on munching away. He never knew that God and Charlie Burke were watching over him.

"Hey, Charlie," Sandra Trilby said, "tell the Douglases what happened to Tony Wyatt up at Big Dipper Lake."

"I dunno," Charlie said, "it was awful." Immediately Bobby wanted to know about it. Without a morning newspaper to rouse my morbid curiosity, I wanted to know, too.

"Go on," Lambert Trilby said, "everything worked out okay. He only lost one arm."

"He *only lost one arm?*" I said.

"Anybody like-a tea?" Reiko said.

"Yeah," Charlie said, "poor Tony—you don't know him, but he's a bush pilot, too—he landed his plane up at Big Dipper Lake. Nobody knows why, but he got out of the cockpit, and somehow the propeller, which was still spinning around, knocked off his right arm."

"*I* wanna tea," Reiko said.

"Yeah," Sandra Trilby said, her multi-rilled old face trying its best to light up into a smile of horrid fascination, "he got knocked into the water, too—and the plane was still moving."

"Is this on the level?" I said.

"Yeah," Charlie said. "Boy! That Tony's got guts. He

grabbed the pontoon rudder just as the plane was pulling away from him and climbed back inside."

"What about his arm?" Bobby said.

"He left it," Charlie said. "He tied a piece of rope around the stump and then around his neck. He had to keep his head pulled way over to the left to keep the rope tight so he wouldn't bleed to death. Then he flew out of Big Dipper way down to the Fielding Lumber Camp so they could radio for help."

"He flew the plane with one arm off?" I said.

"Bobby," Reiko said, "why don't you go outside and look for blueberries?"

"They're all gone, Mommy. No more blueberries till next year—"

"How about frogs?" Reiko said.

"How about the guy with one arm off flying the plane?" Bobby said.

"The radio at Fielding's camp was busted, and Tony was bleeding so much they couldn't stop it," Charlie said.

"Yeah," Lambert said, "that's when Fergie Pruitt volunteered to fly poor Tony to the hospital at South Porcupine."

"Yeah," Sandra said, and started to cackle. She cackled so hysterically I thought she was with egg.

"Sandra!" Lambert said, giving her an admonishing karate chop, which at his advanced age didn't amount to much.

"It's funny!" Sandra said. "Fergie Pruitt never flew a plane in his whole life."

"Yeah," Charlie Burke said, "but he did *that* day. He has more guts than anybody ever gave him credit for."

"How could he fly a plane if he'd never flown one before?" I said.

"It was a miracle," Charlie said. "He'd flown with us so much all his life in the bush that he had a general idea of what to do and by God he did it."

"*I* may take up flying," Lambert said, suddenly remembering that Simpkins Soap had made him a semicapitalist. "Might come in handy."

"Yeah," Sandra said, "Tony might get into trouble again and *you* can fly him to South Porcupine!" Then she cackled again and went into one of her choking fits.

I tried to give her a glass of water, but Lambert said,

"Don't worry about Sandra-baby—she'll be all right after she faints. She'll snap right out of it."

Sandra-baby dutifully fainted, and sure enough, fifteen minutes later the gray started coming back to her cheeks.

When we lived down in Connecticut, I was frequently irritated and annoyed by television's cigarette commercials—not because people are smoking themselves to death, but because the settings chosen to depict the gay, carefree smokers always seemed to be in the deep forest. Now, of course, when I see these same commercials from *within* the deep forest, they make my blood run cold. I just know that these amateur smokers will casually toss their burning butts away without a second thought and ten minutes later the whole countryside will be ablaze. I wish that the advertising agency geniuses who give birth to these alfresco productions would take it that one step beyond their ultimate goal and show the boy and the girl, their hair ablaze, fleeing for their lives from the inferno they have smoked themselves into. Or maybe each pack of cigarettes should be stamped: "Caution: Forest Fires May Be Hazardous to Your Health."

Cigarettes, or the lack of them, almost caused a backwoods murder at our Lost Lake paradise. Jake Moon, the Mr. Joyboy of the North, had gone to Chinookville to have something treated. I didn't ask what this time because he had long since run out of ailments and I didn't want to embarrass him, or maybe I was too busy working to take the time to embarrass him, which is more like it. I had come to enjoy embarrassing him. Back in the bush it doesn't take much to amuse.

Jake was supposed to be back at camp a little after dark, using the light of our television set to guide him across the lake. This is something that should be in every lighthouse in the world—the light from a 21-inch television screen can be seen many times farther than the light from an 8 billion-candlepower light in a lighthouse, but that is another story. Jake did not return a little after dark or a lot after dark, as I knew he wouldn't. Part of the cure for any and all of his afflictions was a few hours at some friendly neighborhood bar, but he usually made it back some time during the night even without the guiding light of the TV set. How he drove that road and steered across the lake in his disarranged condition I'll never know, but somehow he always made it. Until this particular night, which was catastrophic, so far as Reiko was concerned, because she had run out of cigarettes.

About 2 A.M. I heard her prowling the house like a busy pack-rat, raking through ashtrays, looking for longish butts. She found one and uttered a low moan of pure joy. After a few minutes she was back in bed sleeping like a sated moon maiden. The next morning she was up at daylight frantically ransacking the whole house for a perhaps forgotten or over-looked pack of cigarettes. Bobby and I pulled the blankets over our heads and feared for our lives as Reiko's search grew more determined and more desperate.

At an opportune moment I crept from my bed to the radio transmitter and called Canada Goose Airways and told them it was an emergency and I wanted ten cartons of cigarettes flown down immediately. I didn't care what brand as long as they could be lighted by a match and puffed. Mr. McArdle said Canada Goose wasn't flying today because of the heavy fog which blanketed almost all Ontario at that moment. I looked out the window and couldn't even see the lake. I went back and burrowed under the blankets. The front door opened and slammed shut and I could hear Reiko's footsteps retreating into the distance. *My God!* I thought. *She's gonna* walk *to Chinookville*. But I was wrong—she went first to Jake's cabin to see if he had anything smokable. Evidently he had run out, too—maybe that's why he went to town. Reiko then proceeded to each and every one of the other cabins and with the same result.

"Let's go fishing," I said to Bobby as I saw Reiko heading back to our house. Bobby and I went fishing in our pajamas, without poles, bait, nets, or anything, but we were safe.

After a while we got hungry and rowed, with muffled oars, back to the house. As we approached the front door, we couldn't hear a sound. It was really quiet. Too quiet, as they say in a Western when the fort is surrounded by blood-thirsty Apaches. When we opened the front door and sneaked in on little cat feet, Reiko was sitting in front of the fire-place. She had a birch twig in her mouth. The other end was smoking. Every once in a while she'd suck on the twig for a moment, then knock off the ash on the end and put the twig back into her mouth. Then I knew what they meant by the *will* to *survive!*

Living in the center of an area teeming with wildlife, such as moose, bear, wolf, fox, lynx, bison, beaver, mink, marten, fisher, and deer, to name a few, you are not conscious of your situation, because most of these animals are shy and it is very seldom that you see one, unless, of course, you spend hours sitting motionless in one place in the bush where these animals have been seen before then, and only then may you get a glimpse of one of them. There are exceptions, of course. Bears will always come to where you throw your garbage, and bison, deer, and sometimes moose can be enticed to a salt lick.

Chipmunks and squirrels and snowshoe rabbits are the only animals we have around close to the camp. They are very tame and show no fear whatsoever when we come along while they are feeding. They just move over a few feet and go right on. So far we've only had one unwelcome visitor from the animal world, and it's only unwelcome by Reiko. She raises hell because we have a bat in the kitchen. And no matter how many times I catch it (with a net) and put it outside, it always gets back in—a relatively uncomplex maneuver because of an open, unused chimney flue in the roof of the kitchen. Reiko wanted me to put a piece of wire screening over this hole, but Bobby screamed so loud about this I just didn't have the heart to do it.

The bat is about the most unobtrusive little thing I've ever seen, and if it didn't move, you'd never know it was there. Most of the time, at night when it should be out with its bat friends eating its share of mosquitoes and other unnecessary insects, it just hangs around the kitchen, upside down, of course, on the edge of one of the cabinets. If you want to open the cabinet door, it inches, good-naturedly, over to the next cabinet and hangs *there*. It doesn't really resent us being in the kitchen at all and holds no grudge against me for unceremoniously netting it and throwing it outside.

At first, after we decided it was an acceptable kitchen decoration, we were worried about Pussycat, the cougar. We thought that she wouldn't be as fascinated and tolerant as we are about the bat, but so far she is. She's leaped halfway up the wall toward it but not really trying too hard, and once or twice she's made it to the top of the kitchen cabinets, where she just sits and purrs (sounding like a Ferrari idling) and watches the bat from a very close range, where if she wanted to, she could just reach out with one quick swipe of her razor claws and spoil the poor bat's whole evening.

With Doggie, the Pomeranian, it's a different story—he's four pounds of fury and would annihilate the bat if he could get anywhere near it. Why is it that the smallest of the species is always the most bellicose? Maybe it's like what the bad-breath ads say—the best defense is a strong offense.

Doggie was really tough, although we didn't know it until the night he got grabbed by the cat owl. We knew that there was this danger with a dog so small because a cat owl, whose taste buds were none too sophisticated when it came suppertime, would swoop down and sink its talons into anything small enough to be carried off.

On this particular evening Doggie had slipped out the door and was sniffing his way around the island, carefully conserving his supply of urine so he'd have enough for the whole trip. I was sitting in the living room admiring an orange-red sunset when I saw the cat owl in a tree, silhouetted against the sky. It became instantly apparent why they are called "cat" owls, because perched on a limb, that's exactly what they look like. Suddenly it dived for the ground and I heard Doggie yelp. I dashed for the front door and to the rescue, which wasn't really necessary. By the time I reached the scene of battle, the owl was teetering on its rear end, dazed and puzzled at this strange turn of events. Rabbits never fought back like this. Doggie was circling the owl and barking furiously. In a moment or so, the owl flew off into the night, shedding a few feathers en route. Doggie chased it until the lake stopped him; then he stood on the shore and barked in the direction the owl had taken for at least fifteen minutes. Neither I nor Doggie would ever forget this bantam battle, and I'm sure the owl won't either. For years, he'll be regaling his children and grandchildren and great-grandchildren with the heroic tale of his encounter with a saber-toothed Pomeranian.

24

THE Trilbys had not visited *us* for almost a month, so we felt we should do something for *them*. Also, because Charlie Burke had inadvertently kept his plane in the *air* on our many trips over the bush, we felt obligated to him, too, so in a moment of foolish enthusiasm, I suggested we all go to a nightclub in Chinookville and celebrate.

"Can I bring my girl?" Charlie asked.

"I thought you were married," Reiko said.

"I am," Charlie said. "That's why I wanna bring my girl."

Lambert and Sandra Trilby had never been to a Chinookville nightclub and were apprehensive. They associated nightclubs with dens of iniquity. They weren't against iniquity, but they were worried about what to wear.

"You got a dress?" I asked Sandra.

"I don't know," she said. "I got married to Lambert in a dress. But that was sixty-three years ago." She stretched her turtle mouth into what she thought was a girlish smile.

"Dig it out," I said.

"I didn't bury it," she said. "I just put it in a trunk."

"I got a tuxedo," Lambert Trilby said. "I can dig it up."

"You remember where you buried it?" Sandra said.

"Sure I do," Lambert said. "I wasn't *that* drunk at the wedding!"

"You were pissed," Sandra said, her reptilian eyes brimming at the bittersweet memory.

"So were you," Lambert said, "really pissed!"

"That was my mother," Sandra said. "She couldn't bear to lose me."

"Yeah," Lambert said, "that's why she lived with us for nineteen years. And she was pissed the whole time!"

This made Sandra sore. "Lambert Trilby," she said, "I've got a good mind to go back to my mother—right now!" She picked up her wet cigar and faked a false start to the door.

"Why *don't* you go back to your mother," Lambert yelled, "and *right now!*"

"I can't," she said.

"Why not?" I said—ever the marriage counselor.

"Because she's still pissed and she'd never recognize me!" Sandra said, dabbing at her nose with a piece of plywood.

I thought it strange that Sandra Trilby—a ninety-year-old lady—would *have* a mother, who was not only still alive, but still strong enough to pick up a shot glass, but I had the good taste and sense not to delve further into this miracle.

"Then it's all set," I said. "We'll all meet at the Empire Room of the Chinookville-Hilton next Saturday night. Okay?"

Next Saturday night turned out to be the rainiest Saturday night in the history of mankind. The trip across the lake to our soggy Land Rover was one long bailing operation, which never removed more than one-quarter of the water sloshing over our shiny-new going-to-town shoes.

In connecting up the battery in the Rover, everything was so wet I almost electrocuted myself, and later, sliding and skidding down the hairy timber road, I wish I had. And the Rover's headlights were helpless against the downpour. A Greek marathon runner with a damp torch would have given more light and also something to guide us, because the road was just a rumor so far as visibility was concerned.

Route 365 was not much better and the two one-way bridges which traversed the now-wild, raging Chinookville River undulated ominously. Bear droppings mixed with rain gave the tire tread nothing to grab, and driving through this superslippery mess bestowed on us the overall feeling of confidence one gets while iceboating with a drunk. On a lake not quite frozen over.

When we reached the Trans-Canada Highway, with its thundering multi-ton tractor-trailers, driving faster than the speed of sound, plus the usual Saturday night daredevils, playing chicken and dying, we breathed a sigh of gratitude and relief. We were safe at last.

Reiko and Bobby and I were the first to arrive at the Empire Room and were shown an easily arranged ringside table. The room was small and the decor consisted mainly of dusty balloons badly in need of air and long streamers of lifeless twisted paper streamers, strung across the black, greasy-looking ceiling. Apparently the Empire Room had once been used, back in Chinookville's frontier days, to smoke hams and bacon, because the air still had a slightly porcine flavor. Not unpleasant, but hardly a Mardi Gras aroma.

Four aboriginals were chained to the bandstand, where they twanged, banged, pounded and plucked a guitar, drums, piano-organ, and bass violin. These apes were not long from the mother tree, and with the proximity of our ringside table, which I was beginning to regret, they gave off a strong indication that Alpo played a major role in their dietary laws. Alpo laced with hot buttered gin.

Two go-go girls, who had seen better days—but God knows when or where—were caged on each side of the bandstand. Looking at them—even casually, which was all they deserved —I was surprised to see a pan of water and a half-eaten can of salmon in one of the cages. At least, I thought, *someone* cares.

The go-go girls were much too arthritic to keep up with the rock group, and their scanty costumes revealed a rainbow of varicose veins in their pipe-stem legs. Until they started to do what *they* thought was an exciting shimmy, I had no idea they were topless. Their breasts were like dusty wind socks at an abandoned Arizona airport. And the wind wasn't blowing east or west or north or south. No matter how hard these Medicare houris tried to shimmy up a breeze, their wind sock bosoms remained listless at half-mast. Still in mourning for McKinley. Or maybe Lincoln.

Sandra Trilby was the first to arrive. She warped up to our ringside table like she was docking a full-rigged schooner. I was so astonished at her array of finery I didn't recognize her. I just sat in my chair and gaped. She was wearing her ancient wedding gown, which had been drastically shortened to a mini-skirt, revealing her knees, which had been left there by the glacier. Her legs were difficult to describe. She was neither bowlegged nor knock-kneed. Sandra Trilby had one of each. And apparently she was wearing a mammoth-skin body stocking—hair side out. Her mackinaw was thrown carelessly over her shoulders like a stole, and she was using a lorgnette with one lens missing to size up the room and the rest of Chinookville's jet set. In the dim light, I thought she was wearing a human bone through her nose in the style of a New Guinea headhunter, but it turned out to be her wet cigar, which had been smashed in the revolving door as she entered this charming Chinookville *boîte*. I was disappointed.

"Where's Lambert?" I said.

"Oh, he's parking the sled," Sandra said. "And tying up the dogs."

"Sled!" I said. "Whaddya mean?"

"Sorry," she said, her reptilian eyes darting around the room to see who was there. "It's been so *long* since we've been to the city. Not since our wedding day."

"You're kidding," I said.

"No, I'm not," she said. "Lambert and I are really married."

"I didn't mean *that*," I said. "I meant—"

"Lambert and I lived together for eight years before we decided to make it legal," Sandra said, charmed by her own daring admission. "We got married right after the monkey came."

"What?" Reiko said.

"Yes," Sandra said, "my brother sent us a little pet monkey from South America and we decided it wouldn't be fair to him for us to be living in sin."

"What's 'living in sin'?" Bobby wanted to know.

"It's a town near here," I said.

"It's not there anymore," Sandra said.

Before things got really puzzling to all of us, Lambert Trilby suddenly was sitting with us, wearing a tuxedo which was badly in need of mowing. He had shaved for the occasion and his face looked like someone had been playing ticktacktoe with Band-Aids.

"You should use a safety razor, Lambert," I said.

"I got a safety razor," Lambert said, "but Sandra always uses my blade to shave her legs."

"Why doesn't she use sheep clippers?" suggested Charlie Burke, who had just shown up, wearing his Sunday suit and followed by a lady in pink, who looked as if she had only seen the sun in travel folders.

"Couldn't bring Lily," Charlie whispered to me. "They switched her to the night shift at the cannery." Then he said, aloud, "This is my wife, Agnes—say hello to all the nice people."

Agnes didn't open her mouth. She just sat down in the proffered chair and stared straight ahead into her apparently black future. The waitress, who could have been Charlie Burke's wife's twin sister, stood by for our order.

"Why ain't *you* topless?" Lambert said to her.

"Whaddya want to drink?" The waitress sighed.

"I'll betcha you got more than *they* have," Lambert said, indicating the cage creatures.

"Whaddya want to drink?" the waitress repeated.

"How about champagne? Champagne for all of us!" I said, carried away by the spirit of Carnival time.

"We can't serve no intoxicating liquor to nobody under sixteen," the waitress said, secretively indicating Bobby.

"He'll have hot chocolate," I said.

"How old is he?" the waitress said.

"Do you have to be a certain age to drink hot chocolate?" I said.

"Yeah," she said, "they gotta lot of crazy laws in Ontario —I'll bring him champagne. And maybe a little bourbon for a chaser."

"Wanna dance?" Lambert Trilby said, and before Sandra could open her turtle mouth, Lambert was out on the dance floor with Charlie's zombie wife. The missing links were playing something that sounded like mood music for a highway accident and Lambert and his ninety-year-old body started to imitate the other imitators on the dance floor. He did the Swim, the Frug, the Watusi, the Boogaloo, and the Varsity Drag. His partner, Mrs. Burke, remained catatonic and danced to a different drum, but this didn't bother Lambert—he was in business for himself and, despite his years, outlasted everyone else on the floor, and apparently won a cup, which he proudly brought back to the table.

"Look," he said, "I won a cup for dancing. Hey, I'm beginning to like this night life stuff." Then to Charlie Burke's Agnes, he said, "Hey, baby, maybe we could work up an act and go on the road!" Agnes just sat there, waiting for the embalmer.

"Look, Sandra, look at this cup—it's engraved and everything!" Sandra lifted her war surplus lorgnette and peered at the engraving, then read slowly, "Mr. and Mrs. Chico Lopez —Best Waltzers—Harvest Moon Ball, 1922—"

"So it *isn't* new," Charlie Burke said. "It's the first time Agnes ever got a cup for anything."

"What's Agnes got to do with it?" Lambert demanded.

"She was your partner, remember," Charlie said, in a tone which suggested that he had had a few belts before braving the ordeal of going on the town with his wife, instead of Lily, the belle of the Chinookville Fish Cannery.

"Wait a minute," I said, "before there's an argument—why don't you share the cup? Lambert can keep it for six months and then Agnes can keep it for six months—how does that sound?"

"What about Mr. and Mrs. Chico Lopez?" asked Reiko.

"To hell with them," Lambert said. "They're not Canadians."

"Neither are we," Bobby said. "We're Americans."

"Yeah," Lambert said, "but you're different—you're *nice* Americans."

"Thank you," I said, "you're nice *Canadians*."

After a couple of hours of telling each other how nice we all were, we switched from champagne to whiskey—all except me, Bobby, and Reiko. Reiko drank tea and Bobby drank Shirley Temples, a drink to take the place of booze for children, guaranteed to make them throw up. So far Bobby had managed to hold his Shirley Temples very well.

"When the hell's the floor show?" Charlie said as the whiskey began to take hold.

"Yeah," said Sandra, "I'm gettin' sick of them goddamn go-go dancers. They don't do nothin'! And what the hell are they wearin' on the top anyway?"

"Nothing," I said. "They're topless."

Sandra controlled a gastronomical revolt, but released a burp which could only be described as Wagnerian and adjusted her one-eyed lorgnette, to focus it better on the go-go grandmother nearest our table.

"My God," Sandra said, "what are those things filled with —dried peas?" Sandra-baby could have been right. The rock group was playing a samba, and every toss of their tired bosoms sounded like maracas.

Charlie started to rap on his glass with a spoon and yelled, "We want the floor show! We want the floor show!"

"Cool it, Buddy," a young Primo Carnera said, tapping Charlie's shoulder with a 12-inch forefinger. Charlie hadn't had enough to drink yet to challenge this impertinence, but I had the feeling that at any time now he would be ready.

Lambert and Sandra-baby were necking like ninety-year-old teen-agers. They were fumbling for each other in Braille, and if they ever found each other, I'm sure they would have forgotten what they were looking for. Charlie Burke's wife, Agnes, was now the color of a slate quarry in December, and I felt that somehow, during the evening, she had been secretly mummified. Charlie's request for entertainment was soon gratified and sooner regretted.

With a ragged roll on the drum, the Empire Room of the Chinookville-Hilton was proud to present Herbie Hackett— your master of ceremonies! Herbie Hackett proved to be a dour little man, in a loud lapeled tuxedo and with the most phony laugh I have ever heard. He welcomed us to the Empire Room like an insolvent undertaker who had just received a windfall from a nearby airplane crash. Then he told a few jokes from King Tut's jokebook, to which the audience reaction was hysterical. Herbie Hackett was the funniest man in the world, and he was right here in Chinookville! Life was worth living, after all. Herbie, encouraged by this reception, became bold and did a few imitations of Jimmy Cagney, Edward G. Robinson, and Eddie Cantor. The audience was ecstatic. And when Herbie very quickly ran out of his meager supply of talent, he introduced the Empire Girls! They must have been from the empire of the Eugénie period, because if anything, they were older and less athletic than the aged go-go girls. They danced in their idea of unison and ended like the June Taylor Dancers on the Gleason show in the inevitable high kicker routine, which carried them off-stage. Some of them, I thought—permanently.

Next, Herbie had a surprise for us—a hypnotist who asked for volunteers from the audience. He turned down Charlie Burke's wife, because there wouldn't have been enough transition, but he picked Lambert Trilby. The hypnotist, Professor Helber, was either a poor judge of subject, or else the Empire Room limited his choice, because Lambert Trilby turned out to be the least controllable subject, hypnotist-wise, I had ever seen.

Professor Helber got him into enough of a trance so that

he might be placed suspended in midair by two chairs, and he did not break in two when three hard-rock miners from the audience sat on his midsection, but when Professor Helber had Lambert go through the crowd kissing every blonde, he ran into a snag. Lambert dutifully kissed every blonde in the room except his wife, Sandra. When Professor Helber asked him why he didn't want to kiss Sandra, Lambert answered in a voice that sounded like an echo chamber, "I'm not *that* hypnotized!"

At this slur on her Jean Harlow wig and her Mae Murray bee-stung lips, Sandra was all for packing the whole celebration in and heading back to Starvation Lake and a good winter-long pout, but Lambert said he was only kidding, and of all the girls in the world, including Jenny Lind and Annette Kellerman, and Anna Held and Lillian Russell, he loved Sandra-baby the best.

"Are you sure," Sandra said, "you love me better than Lillian Russell?"

"She was nothing," Lambert said. "Big tits, tiny waist, big beautiful ass—nothing."

This assured Sandra, and the party and the floor show continued. Herbie Hackett had another surprise for us— Bubbles Lamour, the singing bubble dancer!

Bubbles Lamour came out nude, with only a tiny Star of David strategically pasted at a strategic location. Bubbles *did* sing. She sang "Deep in the Heart of Texas" while she gyrated in back of the privacy of her enormous bubble, but every time in "Deep in the Heart of Texas" when it came to the handclapping part, she would bounce her bubble high in the air, giving us an unrestricted view of her sparkling Star of David, and clap her hands clap-clap-clap-clap! Then the Star of David would be eclipsed by the latex moon, and the audience would wait with bated breath until the next handclap.

Along about the twenty-seventh chorus of "Deep in the Heart of Texas" and the one hundred and eighth eclipse, Lambert Trilby had had enough.

"Take it off," he yelled.

This suggestion wasn't too specific and the bubble dancer looked puzzled, until someone touched her bubble with a lighted cigarette, and Lambert shouted again, "Take it off!" This time he was on firmer ground.

"I cannot take it off," the bubble dancer said.

"A religious fanatic," someone else said.

"I cannot take it off," the bubble dancer repeated, "but I will do something else." A low murmur of animal anticipation filled the room.

"Watch," the bubble dancer said, and then she pressed her belly button and the Star of David lighted up. Then she blew a kiss to Lambert and fled the floor.

"Golly!" Lambert said. "I wonder where she keeps the batteries?"

"Where do you keep *your* batteries?" Sandra said, fumbling for Lambert again.

"Shall we go home and find out?" Lambert said, trying, I'm sure, to remember the bubble dancer, while cupping the vast area in which Sandra's right breast might have been.

I felt we all should have made the move to leave, but Charlie Burke would have none of it. "Agnes is having too much fun," he said, indicating his unborn wife, who had long ago solidified. "Besides," he added, "I wanna wait for Hildegarde."

"Hildegarde!" I said. "She's never appeared in Chinookville in her life, and she never will!"

"You're certainly a lousy Catholic," Charlie said. "You oughta go to confession first thing in the morning."

"I'm an Episcopalian," I said. "What the hell would I do at confession?"

"Confess you're not a Catholic," he said. "Now let's all settle back and enjoy Hildegarde."

It took me hours to convince Charlie that he'd better revise his dream and that there was a better chance of Marie Antoinette's showing up before Hildegarde.

"Let's wait for her then," Charlie said.

"She doesn't sing," I said, grabbing at straws.

"Maybe she'll hum a little."

I asked the waitress for the check, just as Lambert gave Sandra a kiss of fire, and they both toppled off the Empire Room's rickety chairs and crashed to the floor.

"Wow!" Sandra said.

"I think my lips are broken," Lambert said.

"Everything all right, folks?" asked the young Primo Carnera, in a tone that suggested that it had been too quiet an evening and that bouncing someone out of the joint might be fun.

"Everything's fine," Reiko said.

"What's that on the floor?" young Primo asked.

"Oh," said Charlie, "that's our laundry. There's an all-night laundromat over on Elm Street and—"

"What happened to *her?*" young Primo said, indicating Charlie's wife.

"Oh," Charlie said, "that's the little woman. Thought I'd give her a little recreation. Good to get away from the house and the kids once in a while. Besides, Lily couldn't make it tonight, she had to work."

"Lily?" young Primo said. "You mean Lily Laduc?"

"Not so loud!" Charlie said. "My wife might *not* be dead!"

Young Primo became semijovial. "Lily's a lot of laughs, ain't she?" he said.

"Yeah," Charlie said, but anyone could see that Lily's Dow-Jones had just lost seven points.

"Well, have fun, folks," young Primo said. Then, daintily prodding Lambert and Sandra who still lay in an untidy heap, he added, "You'll never get *them* clean."

"That'll be thirty-four dollars and sixty-five cents," the waitress said. "The sixty-five cents is the entertainment tax."

"Where's Hildegarde?" Charlie said.

"That's what I'd like to know," the waitress said. "Sixty-five cents is a lot of tax for the kind of entertainment we've got."

"Why don't you sit down and have a drink?" Charlie said.

"I'd love to," the waitress said, "but us Bunnies aren't allowed to drink with the customers."

After the waitress left, the Trilbys joined our table again, and Charlie said, indicating the waitress, "*I* didn't know she was a *Bunny.*"

"She's dressed like Martha Washington," Lambert said.

"Martha Washington was the father of our country," Bobby said.

"That's right, Bobby," I said, "and who was the mother?"

"Hildegarde," Charlie said.

"Yeah," Bobby said.

Standing in a downpour in front of the Chinookville-Hilton, with its imposing false-front façade giving hint of the opulence within its walls, we said our good-nights and promised each other we must make this an annual affair. Sandra and Lambert Trilby staggered off to find their borrowed car, and Charlie explained that he'd better hit the sack because he was flying to Povungnituk first thing in the morning, at the same time holding Agnes like he was halfway through a flagpole raising.

"Good night, Charlie," I said, then to Agnes, "Good night, Mrs. Burke, I hope you had a good time."

Agnes showed no sign of responding, so Charlie shook her a little. "Agnes," he said, "the Douglases are leaving—say good night. Thank them for a lovely evening."

Suddenly, and for no apparent reason, Agnes half smiled and said, "Charlie's taking *me* to the Empire Room tonight because Lily's on the night shift at the cannery."

"Come on, Agnes!" Charlie said, then to me, "Poor Agnes —she just can't hold her liquor."

"But—she didn't have a drink," Reiko said.

"I know," Charlie said, "I know." Then he strapped the rigid Agnes to the ski rack on top of his Chevy coupe and drove off toward the lights of the Chinookville Fish Cannery.

"Gee," Reiko said, "just like Connecticut."

25

ONE evening after vespers, Reiko had informed me that she was pregnant.

Bobby was now seven years old. For seven years we had lived within shouting distance of a doctor and the world's greatest medical facilities. Now, when we were 116 miles away from anything remotely Lysolical, my sweet little Japanese angel was going to have a b-a-b-y.

"Has anyone ever told you that you have great timing?" I said.

"No," Reiko said, "only beautiful legs. *You* never tell me I have beautiful legs."

"Why do we have to have a baby *now?*" I said. "Why couldn't we wait until we move to the Antarctic or northern Greenland or until we get shipwrecked on some South Pacific island—a thousand miles from any shipping lanes? Then you and your beautiful legs could have a baby!"

"What's that mean?" Reiko said. "Don't you want a little daughter?"

"Sure I want a little daughter," I said. "But where's the guarantee? How do you know you're gonna have a girl?"

"My grandmother," she said.

"Your grandmother knows you're gonna have a girl?" I said. "How does your grandmother know?"

"She told me when I was small in Japan, 'If sun go down in west, gonna be a girl.'"

"That's brilliant," I said. "The sun *always* goes down in the west."

"You sure?" Reiko said, and the way she said it, I started to waver.

"Yes," I said, very unpositively. "Look," I said, guiding her to our large picture window in the living room which faced exactly west, "you see those very tall pine trees, over there on the edge of the lake? You see the tallest one where that raven just landed—that's west."

"What's a raven?"

"It's that big goddamn black bird that just landed in that big goddamn pine tree!" I said, forgetting for a moment that I was a Dale Carnegie graduate.

"I'm going back Japan!" Reiko said. She says this every time we get loud to each other, which is never less than eight times a day. Sunday is good for twice that number. I don't know why.

I decided to forgo the fun of a good fight this time, so I said, "I want a little girl and I just hope your grandmother knows what she's talking about and forget about the raven."

Reiko wasn't going to let everything drop like that and it

apparently seemed like a dandy time to go mysteriously Oriental and deviously inscrutable.

"Why do you want a little girl?" she said.

"I don't want a little girl," I said. "This is your grandmother's idea."

"You'd rather have another wolf, or a coyote, or a fox. You keep talking about those white foxes," she said.

"I don't keep talking about those white foxes at all. I merely said I would like to have one, and also I would like to have a white wolf—for Father's Day. Never *once* did I mention a coyote."

"You love animals more than you do Bobby and me," she said, demonstrating that women are the same the world over. No matter which way their eyes slant, their brains all tilt the same. If you're a female, you have a congenital jealousy of anything which takes the form of a rival. Be it the husband's job, a shiny new car upon which he lavishes his Sunday attentions, or a dog. Or a white fox. It can also be a favorite television show. Or his stamp collection. His bowling night. Or the blonde next door. I don't know how it is with other normal husbands, but in all my years of living, and in all the places I've lived, the "blonde next door" was always a *man,* who sold used septic tanks.

Reiko seemed to resent, if only occasionally, the time I spent with our animals. And with wild animals, you have to give them time. All wild animals, if you are to keep them friendly and trusting, must be treated like retarded children. They must be constantly loved and petted and handled and cuddled and reassured. This will not domesticate them, but it will prevent them from suddenly ripping you, their natural enemy, to bloody bits. Come to think of it, a wife should be treated the same way—for the same reason.

Soon after Reiko's announcement of her sneaky pregnancy, I started to, as Custer must have, take stock of the situation. Although we were 116 miles from a doctor and a hospital, when the time drew near for her to add to the good Reverend Malthus' problem, we would simply move into Chinookville in advance and just wait until the baby arrived. There would be no midnight dash to the hospital or any of that kind of carryings-on. My three weeks in the Boy Scouts, back when Dan Beard was running the show, had taught me one thing: "Be Prepared!" Actually my three weeks in the Boy Scouts had taught me *two* things. The other was: "No Drinking at Jamborees!"

One of the books I had brought with me into the bush was the Boy Scout *First Aid*. I thumbed through it, in secret, so as not to alarm the future mother of the future Jackie Onassis, Princess Grace, or Myra Breckinridge. There was nothing in the BS *First Aid* booklet that said anything about childbirth. Apparently there were no merit badges for this. I didn't find out a few other things that I'm sure will stand me in good stead someday; for instance, I learned nothing of what to do in case of ticks. "Ticks," the section devoted to them read, "are usually harmless, but you can't be sure." I stopped reading this right then. I will have nothing to do with indefinite afflictions.

Other chapters in the booklet were equally fascinating and considerably more horrifying. I skimmed mostly because I didn't really want to know about bleeding blisters, burns, choking, dislocations, drownings, electrocutions, epileptic seizures, fractures, gunshot wounds, hiccups, lockjaw, poisoning, snakebites, tetanus, and simple elephantiasis. All I wanted to know, in Reiko's condition, and our singular location was "What to Do if the Doctor Ain't Coming."

Another not helpful book which I have on my sagging shelves is *The American Illustrated Medical Dictionary,* which was willed to me by my late Uncle John, an ear, nose, and throat specialist, who spent most of his twilight years fixing up *my* nose, which was constantly being altered at Stillman's Gym, the old Pioneer A.C., and the old Markwell Bar, a murky dungeon underneath the old Markwell Hotel on Forty-ninth Street, where Harry Golden once night-clerked for his brother, who owned the trap. It may not be much, but it's as close as I ever got to rubbing elbows with greatness. It pains me somewhat now to know that I will probably never know Harry Golden, and I will go to my maker (who put me together *all wrong!*) forever kicking my ass that I never troubled to find out who the night clerk was at the old Markwell Hotel, but from *now* on, I'm investigating every night clerk in *every* old hotel. I may run across Zane Grey or Clare Boothe Luce.

But back to dear Uncle John's legacy—it was loaded with medical goodies, illustrated by ghastly drawings of every affliction known to man, or at least to the sadist who compiled this 1,493-page compendium of horrors, all the way from "ā a a disease. Chlorosis aegyptiaca, the hookworm infection of the Ebers Papyrus (Joachim); also thought to be bilharziasis, since the hieroglyph is a phallus," to "zygospore. A spore formed by the conjugation of two cells (gametes) which are morphologically identical and do not show any sexual differentiation," either of which would make an ideal structural base on which to build a successful television series with Omar Sharif and Mama Cass or a new religious order.

Actually the only real nitty-gritty information I could find in the whole book was a column and a half describing the symptoms of pregnancy, with a side-view drawing of a woman in what must have been her twenty-third month. Either that or she had been cornered by an uptight palomino stallion out back of Roy Rogers' barn. Or in Roy Rogers' motel (they have very high ceilings). This kind of artwork, I could see immediately, would be of no real benefit if Reiko suddenly started having a litter, during a January blizzard, with no hope of even reaching a filling station with a sterile attendant, let alone a hospital.

I have two other books, which I thought essential for my backwoods health plan. One, *First Aid for Animals*, just didn't cut the mustard when it came to a pregnant human being, and the other, *The Merck Manual*, a dandy 1,850-page tome, was again too explicit for a cowardly lion like myself. After I had read the chapter on "Complications of Pregnancy," I decided that maybe being the father of a future sneaky conglomerate, which would take over not only big business but the Mafia as well, wasn't so important after all.

I placed my medical library back on the shelf and went outside and walked through the woods to a solitary point of land, jutting into the lake, where I faced the east and prayed. I prayed to my God and also to Manitou, the god of the Algonquin Indians. I felt that if they both helped, everything would work out fine. I directed a few *extra* words to Manitou, because, after all, this is his territory.

Reiko's pregnancy was normal, and after a while I became less apprehensive of the big day ahead. There were a few moments of minor crises. Pregnant Caucasian women are prone to wild taste fancies such as pickles and strawberries at very odd hours and they almost collapse into terminal delirium tremens if these unprocurable delicacies are not forthcoming. With Reiko there was none of this nonsense. All she wanted at twelve midnight was fried octopus. I didn't know what to do about this. Even if I could have flown to Chinookville, at this dark hour, I don't think I would have had the guts to wake up Pierre Lachaise of Lachaise's Food-mart. Pierre had been at Dienbienphu and somehow suspects that Reiko is related to the little Tonkinese B-girl who stole his gold watch at a go-go joint in downtown Hanoi. In 1954.

I couldn't understand Reiko's frenzied penchant for fried octopus, no matter how pregnant she got. I've tried fried octopus. It's like eating Keds.

The new baby was due during the third week in January, so I made arrangements for us all to stay at the Malemute Motel in Chinookville until the pains started. Jimmy Horse, the Indian trapper whose trapline came within two miles of our camp, agreed to snowmobile over and feed the animals while we were gone. I hated to leave them for that long, but the Malemute Motel had strict rules: "No smoking in bed and no dogs, no wolves, and no cougars," which, of course, is discrimination at its worst.

We had planned a very quiet Christmas at home. Reiko wanted to know, "Where we gonna get a Christmas tree?" —a question, I felt, calling for an extremely controlled answer, as I looked out the front window at the millions and millions of pine, balsam, spruce, and white fir trees which surrounded Lost Lake for perhaps a thousand miles. And more.

"Maybe," I said, "maybe we could go out into the woods and cut our very own Christmas tree. Wouldn't that be fun?"

"Papa," Bobby said, "it's thirty-five below zero today. Don't you remember? We heard it on the radio."

"The marmalator says forty below," Reiko said, "marmalator" being my spelling of her version of "thermometer."

"We don't have to go today," I said. "Maybe it'll be warmer tomorrow."

We waited for a few days until the mercury climbed to 25 below, and then we snowmobiled a short distance into the woods to look for a little pine tree. Despite the low tempera-ture, it didn't seem any colder than it had back in Old New Litchridge at 10 above, because the air was much drier, and it smelled a lot better. I never understood the cliché "air like wine" until we came up here. It was not intoxicating, but the exhilaration it distilled was almost beyond description. I felt twenty years younger—until Reiko pointed out the beautiful balsam fir tree she wanted me to cut down. I aged immediately. It must have been 30 feet tall.

"That's a good one, Papa," Bobby said, his warm sweet breath forming an icy halo over his wolf fur hood.

"Yeah," I said, "why don't we leave it here—'cause that's just where it would be even if I could cut it down—with this *dull* ax [I threw that in for good measure]?"

"Why?" Reiko asked.

"Because we couldn't possibly get it back to camp. The snow is too deep."

"I'm strong," Reiko said.

"Sure you are," I said, "but you're gonna have a baby any hot second and the doctor told you not to lift any thirty-foot Christmas trees."

"Papa?" Bobby said, "how is Santa Claus gonna find us way back here in the woods?"

"Easy," I said, at the same time thinking how wonderful it was that he still *believed* in Santa Claus.

"Maybe he'll just fly on by and won't see our house."

"Sure he will," I said. "I'll run a flag up on the flagpole, and then he'll know we're here."

"What kind of a flag?" Bobby said.

"The Canadian flag. This is Canada."

"But we're Americans."

"Okay, we'll run up the American flag, too."

"What about Mommy? Have we got a Japanese flag?"

"We don't need one—Mommy's an American now."

"She *still* looks Japanese," Bobby said.

"I know," I said, "but give her a little time—she's new at it."

"The baby just kicked my stomach," Reiko said. "I think it's cold."

The sun had disappeared completely, and the sky looked suspiciously like it was conjuring up a snowstorm.

"Why don't we go back to camp?" I said. "We can all have a nice cup of coffee to put our hands in; then we can go right outside in our own front yard and decorate one of the pine trees there. There's no rule that says a Christmas tree has to be in the house."

We finished decorating the tree at dusk. I started the

generator and suddenly, accompanied by shrieks of childish pleasure from Bobby and Reiko, the little pine tree came ablaze with a hundred or more blue, twinkling yellow, green, pink, and red lights, standing alone with a pastel background of blue snow covering the vast expanse of the frozen Lost Lake. Its brilliant beauty was breathtaking. The little islands were black and mysterious. The northern lights flamed up for thousands of miles into the polar sky and, almost instantly, disappeared. There was a distant mournful sound of a lonely wolf, then the soft hiss of snow. It was *really* Christmas Eve.

At twelve midnight Reiko started to have labor pains.

26

THIS is Mrs. Mike *all over again,* I thought as I tried for the tenth time to start the engine on our number one snowmobile. *Mrs. Mike* was a terrifying best seller about the almost impossible hardships of life in the far north, and it had been written by my friend Benny Friedman, who used to work on the Red Skelton show with me a few years ago. Where Benny Friedman got all his information about life in the frozen north was a mystery. He had never been out of the Beverly Hills at that time, but his story had been extremely graphic— especially the chapter which dealt with the birth of a baby in a tiny ice-cube-lined cabin somewhere around the Arctic Circle in the dead of winter. His description of the woman's screaming agony and the husband's crushing helplessness all came back to me now. Why the hell couldn't I remember something like *Rebecca of Sunnybrook Farm* or *Moby Dick* or *My Brother Was an Only Child?*"

I yanked savagely again at the Ski-doo's pull cord and praise God the engine burst into a rattling machine-gun start, which was barely audible over the shrieking wind. I looked down at my hands in the yellow glow of a 25-watt bulb hanging over me in the snowmobile shed. They were a study in red and white. White where my fingers were starting to freeze solid and red where I had bled myself on the ice-stiffened pull cord. In the panic I felt at the ever-diminishing time between Reiko's contractions I had forgotten to put on my mittens. I floundered through deep snow back toward the house. The lovely gentle snowstorm of a few hours before was now a vicious, man-killing blizzard; the tiny, ice-hard pellets of snow were tearing at my face and my bare hands like thousands of infinitesimal needles. My hands were numb, but my face felt like it was being eaten alive by a vast horde of invisible piranhas. The struggle up the small hill to the door of the lodge combined with the strength of the gale left me without breath. I fell through the front door into an untidy heap in the middle of the living-room floor. A polar bear head grinned a yellow-toothed grin six inches away from my shredded face. At that moment, I wouldn't have cared if it had been alive and well—I was happy to get back into the house.

Reiko moaned and held her belly and Bobby said, "Papa, the hockey game is still on. You wanna watch it? Montreal is ahead three."

"Bobby," I said, regaining some of my wind, "how brave are you?"

"I'm the fastest runner in the whole school," he said.

"Look," I said, "the radiophone isn't working, so I've got to take Mommy to the hospital."

"I wanna go, too," he said, trying to make his lower lip like Jackie Cooper used to make.

"Bobby," I said, "we can't fool around arguing—it's too cold outside for you." It was too cold for any of us. The thermometer read minus 25, and with at least a 35-mile-per-hour wind, the chill factor would put the temperature down to 90 below. I didn't dare add the speed of the snowmobile, which would make it even lower. When I adopted Emerson's advice as a sort of an unsolicited standard pattern for my life, I didn't know I was going to have so many opportunities to do something I was afraid to do. Right now I had to cross three miles of blizzard-swept lake in the middle of what looked like the darkest night of the century, with a woman who was with child, but with the acceleration of her moans— I knew that the child wasn't long for with *her*.

Reiko, who by this time no longer spoke, just sat crouched there like a wounded doe watching me—wondering if I were going to help her or finish her off. Getting her dressed developed into an admixture of tenderness and cruelty: the tenderness I felt for her almost utter helplessness and the cruelty with which I had to insist on certain cumbersome garments, which were the only things which would keep her alive until we reached help. Bobby, sensing the urgency of the situation and knowing all along that I would take him, got dressed without asking for any help, for the first time.

Our number one snowmobile was a 24-horsepower Ski-doo, an extremely powerful machine, and it had to be with the soon to be *four* of us riding her, plus our snowshoes and survival gear, which we always carried—just in case. I had a feeling as we started out across the frozen lake that we weren't heading for Chinookville at all—our objective was Mars, and we would be the first earth skeletons to be found there by the first NASA search party in 1983. A small new obstetrics textbook I had picked up at the Chinookville drugstore and would never have any use for, which I had grabbed on my way out of our cabin, was tucked into the pocket of my second or third shirt, which gave me all the security and comfort a parachute jumper gets when his parachute doesn't open, but when, on the way down, he discovers, to his delight, that he will be landing in a field of daisies.

A blizzard is described by the weather bureau as a severe weather condition characterized by low temperatures and strong winds bearing a great amount of snow (mostly fine dry snow picked up from the ground). To qualify, a blizzard must also have sufficient snow in the air to reduce visibility to less than 500 feet. A *severe* blizzard must have the visibility reduced to near zero, to make good in the "severe" category. Our blizzard was going all out above and beyond the call of the weather bureau.

I had had the foresight, before winter closed in on us, to install flasher lights on four of our thirteen islands, which would guide us in case we were caught out on the ice after dark. These are the same flasher lights the gas company uses to warn New York muggers of dangerous excavations in the streets. They are yellow and can be seen at a great distance, except when the visibility is *lower* than zero, if that term is meteorologically correct. This night proved that there is something darker than black. The flasher lights might just as well have been on a submarine at the bottom of the Marianas Trench. We could see *nothing* but the searing whiteness of the flailing snow in the dim beam of the Ski-doo's headlight. I switched on my Sun Gun, a powerful photographic light we carried for night travel. This only made the night more terrifying. The swirling wall of snow was now rolling over us in viscous waves hundreds of feet high and now in the intense light of the Sun Gun it took on the look of an all-engulfing lava flow that felt at once white hot and bone-crushing cold.

I lost track of time completely. The only clue I had was Reiko's moans, which were coming closer together. Bobby made not a sound. He just straddled the rear of the snowmobile without moving. He looked like a frozen snow statue. I yelled to him above the screaming wind, "Bobby, are you all right?" He didn't answer, so I stopped the Ski-doo and stepped off it to go back to him and check. The minute I stepped off I kept going down. The snow was either up to my armpits or my armpits stopped me from sinking any farther. With more strength than I actually have I managed to pull myself back onto the Ski-doo.

Between groans Reiko asked, "Jack-san, where did you go?"

With my customary ever-ready wit I said, "I went to check the ice to see if it was safe to cross."

Then Bobby yelled, "Papa, are you all right?"

The storm had now reached such a velocity that you had to keep squinting. If you opened your eyes wide, the wind would lift up your eyelids. Even under your goggles.

The previous snowmobile tracks which I had been following had now disappeared under mountainous drifts, which I handled by simply giving the Ski-doo as much gas as possible and gunning it through, leaving a series of long, ragged tunnels in our wake. The snow was that deep.

It might have been minutes or hours—I never knew—but suddenly I saw one of our flasher lights, giving proof through the night that our island was still there. Which island I didn't know. I hoped against hope that it was the one with the little log cabin on it. It wasn't. I knew then and there that if *I* were carrying the serum to Nome, Nome would be in big trouble because we were not going to make it.

Somehow I found a more or less sheltered spot next to a large dark mass which must have been a huge rock and proceeded to set up our Jiffy Survival Tent—which is a very simple operation—if you have the strength of Samson, Atlas, and Vic Tanny, plus the deductive capabilities of Charlie Chan and the unerring dexterity of a stud porcupine. This was the tent, according to the jolly bastard optimist who sold it to me, that was the same type used by Captain Robert F. Scott in his dash to the South Pole. I suddenly remembered, while I was frantically trying to set it up, I don't recall ever hearing about his dashing *back!* It was then that I gave up with the stakes and spring wire poles and strung a rope between two trees, over which I threw the snow-stiffened canvas; I pushed more snow over the edges of the tent, which quickly froze it into a bond with the ground. Then I ran the Ski-doo inside this pitiable wigwam, and after closing the end flaps, by simply holding them for a moment until icy snow glued them permanently together, I lit a small, portable Coleman lantern and put a match to a small, portable Coleman stove, at the same time wishing I had a small, portable Coleman obstetrician. Bobby immediately produced a toy jet plane from somewhere and started zooming it around the little tent. Reiko's contractions were only about six minutes apart now, so I turned the radio on and picked up a hip disc jockey from Sault Ste. Marie who was having the time of his life playing Lorne Greene singing "Bonanza," a 33⅓ rpm recording, which was playing at 78 rpm, making Lorne Greene sound like Donald Duck getting a hi-colonic, which made for great midwife music.

Then I took out my new obstetrics book, and I must say, they got right to it with the first chapter under the heading *"Surprise! Surprise!"* As snow started sifting in through the hole where our used air was supposed to go out, I read: "Unexpected childbirth happens all the time. Don't panic. This is not a unique situation." This immediately made me calmer. After all, what was so unique about it? A man and his wife and his little boy crouching in a little tent during a blizzard, and the wife is about to have a baby, and the doctor is 116 miles away, sleeping peacefully. "Let Mother Nature handle everything." Ah! I was off the hook. "Above all: 1. Don't pull baby or its cord. 2. Tie cord as soon as baby is delivered." With what? A Ski-doo fan belt? "3. Cut cord only if no help is likely." Don't use Ski-doo fan belt. "4. To keep baby warm if the room is cold, place it between the mother's legs." It looked like that's where we'd *all* be before morning.

Reiko was just about ready. She was panting like a hard-run hound, and beads of sweat covered her forehead. I made her lie down on the Ski-doo seat. I pulled off her heavy snowsuit and her thermal underwear, put her boots back on; then I propped her feet up on the handles of the snowmobile and wedged her feet in between the control levers.

Bobby stopped breaking the speed of sound with his jet and looked at me with a weird expression. "What're you gonna do, Papa?"

"Bobby," I said, "I'll be goddamned if I know. When I used to raise pigs, this kinda thing never bothered me."

"Mommy gonna have pigs, Papa?"

"I wish she were," I said. "At least I'd know what to do—but with a baby."

"Little pigs are cute," Bobby said, then took off once again into the wild blue yonder.

I read further in the obstetrics book and started crazily answering it back: "Preparation: Lie mother-to-be on something flat." A snowmobile seat is pretty flat. "Boil scissors." Okay, but how will I know when they're done? "Put mother in best position when bulge appears and birth imminent. Knees up." She had bulged for months, and her knees *were* up.

Reiko shuddered. She was cold. I had been so anxious to get her ready and in position I had neglected to cover her again, so I got two heavy Hudson's Bay blankets and threw them over her raised legs, and then I lit a small can of Sterno and placed it under the blanket. I couldn't help thinking if only this was a *casserole* I was preparing instead of a *mother*.

I felt sure it was almost time, so I quickly read on: "After the baby is born, think of a name for it." What the hell was this? I was in such a state of panic I couldn't think of my *own* name! I flipped the book over to see who wrote it, and *there it was: The Paper Mother!*—with a photograph of George Plimpton, smiling, in a see-through maternity dress.

The howling wind had now reached what had to be the height of its velocity. The little tent bellied in so all four sides almost touched, giving Bobby very little room for taking off and landing. I turned the Coleman lantern a notch to give us some more light and brilliantly turned it off. Now came the search in the pitch-black darkness for matches. I always kept my dry matches in a little round plastic pill container, which could be broken open by crushing it with your feet—this I had learned from Charlie Burke. He said a regular keep-your-matches-dry container had to be unscrewed—a task which would be quite impossible if your hands were frozen or nearly so. My pill container of dry matches was not in my parka pocket or anywhere else that I could feel. I was no longer in a panic. I was passing into the limbo land of shock. What little there was left of my mind raced through a whole, totally appalling catalogue of snowy disasters, starting with the Donner Party, who were trapped by a blizzard in the High Sierra, which turned out to be a Donner dinner party, with the Donners as the main course. I had written jokes about this hilarious tragedy, back in the days when I was writing black comedy for white comics. Now, of course, it's vice versa.

I was about to give up when Bobby said, "Papa, I've got some matches."

Do you think I kissed my sweet little boy with undying gratitude, when he said this? No. I said, *"How* many *times* have I *told* you *not* to play with *matches?"* Why can't I be more like Judge Hardy and less like Jack the Ripper?

After we had light again in our tiny, snow-filled tomb, and just as the demented disc jockey from Sault Ste. Marie started to play a recording of Lorne Greene, with The Supremes, singing "Only God Can Make a Tree," Reiko screamed and made a baby.

Instantly I was calm and cool and all the obstetrical knowledge I had learned when I raised pigs was recalled, and in no time at all, I was organized, and mother and baby were doing fine. Just before she fell into a deep, exhausted sleep, Reiko said, "I'm going back Japan."

27

BACK in Connecticut or New York, Reiko and I would never think of going out on New Year's Eve or giving a party at home. We both felt, as Joe E. Lewis so wisely put it, "New Year's Eve is for amateurs."

Of course, I was always, in recent years anyway, handicapped at *any* kind of party because I've tapered off on the sauce, thus putting myself at the mercy of every lush from Bangor to Burlingame. Nothing disturbs an otherwise happy tosspot quicker than to make the appalling discovery that there is someone, at whatever the jolly group is gathering to celebrate, who is obviously not celebrating. He immediately suspects that you are staying semisober just to spite him *personally*.

"Whatsamatter, Old Buddy"—this spoken in a tone that clashes with "Old Buddy"—"we're not good enough for you to drink with us? Big-shot television star!" (They always get me mixed up with Melvin Douglas—or most of the time, Paul Douglas—who died back in 1959.) Or Donna Douglas. Depending on which earrings I was wearing.

"Oh," I usually say, "you're good enough to drink with, but I don't feel as though *I* am worthy."

The next line, from the drunk, is most always a lard-tongued "What the fuck does that mean?"

Wives, at parties, invariably wind up getting sore at their husbands or vice versa. "Whaddya mean, you were just talkin'? I saw that sonofabitch put his hand on your ass, and you didn't even move!" This line is most commonly directed by the husband to the wife, but sometimes by the wife to the husband (the antique dealer). Another reason we pass up parties: Being reasonably sober, we usually are delegated by a weaving hostess to take either the wife or the husband home, because their mates have flounced out earlier and haven't been seen since. These leftover people never live within the continental United States, and by the time you deliver *them* to their unhappy doorsteps, *you* get home just as Junior is getting on the school bus, minus his breakfast and his shoes and socks.

Living in the backwoods had evidently given us either false courage or it had destroyed our natural wariness of the social life or dimmed our memories, because we decided to have a party. A *New Year's Eve* party.

We had to be careful with the party list, which we immediately started to compile. We could only have more or less affluent people, because of the air fare from New York or California to Chinookville. Friends on welfare were definitely out. They were spending the winter in the Virgin Islands. We also realized that this would be the supreme test of who our friends really *were* and who were really *not*. This made us almost abandon the whole nutty project. I'd rather go to my quiet little grave not knowing which was which, but again, dear Ralph Waldo's words came to mind, so we both decided to do something we were afraid to do.

By the third day of party planning the list was three pages long and growing. Reiko and I both knew this was ridiculous because the guests would have to stay overnight and we only had six livable cabins, plus a dormitory cabin on the second island out in the lake, which we could use in case of emergency—such as party crashers, which wasn't too likely, being so far from town, but you know how news of a good party gets around. And this was going to be a good party. If we got snowed in, it would be a *great* party.

After we got the guest list cut to size, I gave the invitations to Charlie Burke, who, winging his way back from some remoter lake, had dropped in for coffee. Charlie promised to mail them, and soon was bouncing over the icy hummocks of Lost Lake into a last minute cliff-hanger takeoff. I think he did this to impress us and it did.

Ordinarily, I would have used the telephone to invite people to a bash, but in addition to the high cost of long distance, if we went beyond three minutes, and with a radio-phone, there is no such thing as a private line. We shared, as I have mentioned, our channel with fourteen *other* people, who take turns trying to keep us from using *our* phone. This actually didn't take much doing because we are at the tail end of the fringe area and any signal which is transmitted by us when we press the little button on our phone is considerably weaker than our fellow subscribers who are a lot closer to Bell Canada's Chinookville transmitter. Our signal is weaker and apparently slower, so what we had to do, if we wanted to make a call during the daylight hours, was to remove the phone from its cradle and then listen in to whoever was talking and immediately after they said their endless good-byes, we pressed our button which signals the Chinookville mobile operator, and if by some miracle, which very seldom came to pass, we got her ear, we simply gave her our number and the number we were calling, and every one of the other fourteen parties could just sit and listen until *we* were finished. The effect was like trying to sandwich in an appendectomy three minutes before the San Francisco earthquake hit. If you took a breath, you sliced your own umbilical cord to the big mother of the outside world. It might take hours before you could regain what you had lost by being foolish enough to breathe.

Most of the other fourteen subscribers seemed to be lumber company men or miners talking to each other from some inaccessible area or from the bottom of some hole. Then there were the "lovers." They were the *worst.* They would take *hours* to set the time for a rendezvous.

"How about eight o'clock?" he'd say.

"Oh, all right," she'd say.

"Eight thirty better?" he'd say.

"Oh, all right," she'd say.

"Maybe seven thirty?" he'd say.

"Oh, all right," she'd say.

"How about *now?"* I'd say.

My interruption would never disconcert these ardent young lovers (I assumed they were ardent, young, and lovers) and most of the time, they would agree with this suggestion and hang up. Also, there were not too many of the amorously frustrated, because if they needed a radiophone to communicate with each other, they were too far from each other to get together any *other* way. Strange, that with all its technical know-how, the Bell System hasn't yet perfected a reliable electronic Dial-a-Hump system. When they do—and they *will*—they'll pick up a lot more long distance overtime— especially from some of us older folk.

So much for the future communication for the masses, which is much too good for them. We had our New Year's Eve party to think about, and think about it was all we did —night and day. We wanted this to be the perfect party, because we wanted our friends to come back again, but transportation was the big problem. We thought at first, we'd have everybody meet in New York and fly to Lost Lake by a chartered plane, but after learning the price of this whimsy, we dropped the idea like a hot pizza. We finally settled on everybody meeting at the Chinookville Airport, where they would debark from an Air Canada Viscount and jump into the Kerry school bus, which our friend Toomey Sillins, the driver, agreed to convey our distinguished guests from the Chinookville Airport to the junction of Route 365 and the timber road which led to Lost Lake and fun! Fun! Fun!

At 5 P.M. Reiko and I and Bobby and our new baby, Timothy, were waiting at the junction. Reiko, Bobby, and I in our fur parkas and Timothy wrapped in several layers of hot-water bottles and Hudson's Bay blankets. It was the very last day of the old year, and it was dark. Very dark. But it was beautiful. There was no wind and the stars were brighter than I had ever seen them. They were cold and hard and there were millions of them. As we sat there in the velvety blackness, Reiko and I wondered if anybody would show up at all, even though everyone we had invited had accepted. We thought we might wind up like Gloria Swanson in *Sunset Boulevard*—waltzing with each other to the music of the Vienna String Quartet (we had every LP *they* ever made, which had, along with the Land Rover, the moose horns, and the polar bear rug, been part of what we had acquired with the purchase of our woodland retreat).

Because of the increasing cold, and Reiko's slightly shaky condition, owing to her recent successful try at ad lib motherhood, Jake, whom we had pressed into service, much against his better judgment, because of whatever physical weakness he was featuring that week, suggested we make a fire. I suggested that he help gather the firewood and this brought on an attack. From what I didn't try to learn. Even in the beauty of this pristine wilderness, I couldn't help hoping that Jake would come down with something that would give us an excuse to bury him in a lonely grave next to the trail and mark it with a crude cross made of two pieces of split pine with an epitaph burned into the piece at the top, HERE LIES JAKE MOON, WHO DIED FROM EVERYTHING. This whole idea so titivated my sense of romantic tragedy that for a long moment I toyed with the idea of killing him. Of course, it would have to look like an accident so I'd just tell the police that I stabbed him, quite inadvertently, while I was cleaning my knife.

My gay reverie was interrupted by distant tentacles of light feeling their way cautiously along the icy surface of Route 365 across the two one-way bridges that spanned the Chinook River just west of our timber road.

"It's the school bus!" Bobby shouted.

"I hope it isn't empty," Reiko said.

"How could it be empty?" I said. "Somebody's driving it."

"That's funny, Papa," Bobby said.

"Humph!" Jake humphed, and then let go with a belch that sounded like the mating call of a horny moose.

"You sound like a horny moose," I said.

"Thank you," he said, proving once again that there was some lack of communication between us.

The school bus came to a sliding stop, almost sideswiping us and our snow vehicles. A voice came through loud and clear from inside the bus. "Whaddya mean—*this* is *it?* Where the hell are we? At the Pole?"

Reiko and Bobby and I ran around the bus door just as Jack Paar was fighting his way through his camera equipment to the road. When he saw us, he said, "Jack, have you ever thought of moving to Tibet? It's *closer*, you know." Then he kissed Reiko and Bobby, before he was rudely shoved aside by what seemed like an avalanche of people thundering down out of the bus. In the blackness of the frigid Canadian night it was hard to recognize anybody. I hoped we had the right bus. Finally a battery of flashlights appeared and in the cross beams, I saw Randy and Miriam Paar, Merv and Julann Griffin, Johnny and Joanne Carson, Dean Martin (who hadn't shown up at Thanksgiving), Hy and Dorothy Averback, Julie Newmar, Diahann Carroll, Alex and Hildy Cohen, David and Linda Black, and Barbara Eden, her navel, and her husband, the Indian.

In the uncertain light of the bobbing flashlights, it was difficult to make positive identification, but nevertheless, it looked like we were going to have a helluva party and some of it had already started. One guy kept falling down in front of the bus and Toomey Sillins, the driver, had to keep jamming on his brakes, as he attempted to break away from all this pandemonium and get to a party of his own choosing, down at the little fishing village of Kerry, where he lived. The Drunk, as he became immediately known, was apparently a stray, because no one seemed to know who he was, and after Toomey had got his bus safely away, we knew we couldn't leave him in the road to be found sometime in the spring with his frozen bottle in one hand and his Clemson banner in the other. Ontario has a very strict law about littering.

Reiko drove one of the snowmobiles with Bobby and Randy Paar, while Jake, whom I had found behind a bush with the Drunk and a bottle and a guilty look, drove the other snowmobile with his newly found friend and some other loser. I drove the Jesus-5 and pulled a huge old lumber sledge, which I had found some months before on an abandoned bush road. It carried all the other funsters and the luggage with ease. We started down our road with the J-5 and the lumber sledge in the lead. I had given everyone colored safety flares, which they waved around dangerously. A few were dropped into laps, which added to the fun, even though it did create an aura of pungent purple singe around our nutty caravan.

Jake, who must have had more than one pull at the Drunk's bottle, apparently decided that the procession was a little too slow for his daredevil propensities, suddenly pulled out of line and zoomed on past us and promptly hit a hidden snow-covered stump and caromed the Ski-doo off it into a ditch and turned it upside down. Immediately I revived my dream of the lonely trailside grave, which could also have its practical side as a mileage marker, because we were just one mile from Route 365.

Everyone screamed with merriment at the overturned Ski-doo as I knocked the ice from the J-5's winch and prepared to winch it back to the road. Jake, the Drunk, and the other loser were unscathed, as they say everywhere unscathed people gather. I hoped the Ski-doo had emerged the same way. *It* wasn't expendable.

"Whatsamatter, Jack?" Jake said.

"Nothing," I said, "you just hit a stump."

"I can do it *every* time," he said.

"I know," I said, "but you might break the machine."

"What do *you* care?" he said. "*You* got lotsa money. What the hell do you care if I break the machine? You can *always* buy *another one*." Something within me snapped and I took a shovel off the Jesus-5 and walked over to the side of the trail and started digging. Gradually, the singing and shouting and the flare waving stopped.

"What are you doing?" Jake said, his tone suggesting trepidation.

"I'm digging a grave," I said.

"Wow!" someone yelled. "How about *that* for a kinky New Year's Eve bit! A funeral! It's the most original party stunt I ever heard of! Yippee!"

"Whose grave?" Jake said, backing up nervously and tripping over the Drunk.

"Guess," I said, and kept digging in the icy snow until I had a lovely 3- by 3- by 6-foot hole. I thought that was deep enough—for a New Year's Eve. "Come here, Jake," I said. "I wanna try this on for size."

"I think I'll go cut some firewood for the winter!" he shrieked, and made a dive toward the thick forest which lined both sides of the road. The Drunk grabbed him.

"Oh, no, you don't!" the Drunk said. "We don't *like* party poopers up here in the *Yukon!*" He was a little confused about his locale, but his intentions were magnificent. He hammerlocked Jake and led him over to the hole I had dug. The red glow of the safety flares lighted the scene with the eerie luminosity cherished by the Druids during their human sacrifice ceremonies. And Off-Broadway producers during the sodomy scene in *Alice in Wonderland*.

"Let's get it over with—I'm gettin' cold," Merv Griffin said. "Anybody know a good short graveside *Latin* prayer?"

"Maybe he's not Catholic," Johnny Carson suggested.

"Don't worry about that," Jack Paar said. "When he's laid out down in that hole, he'll come around *quick!*"

"Why can't *you* think of fun parties like this?" a voice, which sounded like the Duke of Windsor's, asked.

"Because *you* always want to go to bed early," said another voice, which sounded like the Duchess'.

I felt by then that I had done enough to keep Jake in line, so I fastened the shovel back onto the J-5 and climbed aboard.

"Okay, everybody!" Dean Martin shouted. " 'Silent Night' —hit it!" And as they all swung into this lovely hymn, with a rock beat, Jake and the Drunk and the Loser quietly got onto the snowmobile and we started up again toward Lost Lake and all it had in store for us. This time Jake kept his machine well to the rear of the rest of the party. I don't know whether he was really scared or not, but I suppose that surrounded as he was with *my* gang, he felt *anything* could happen to him way back there in the bush. I would have had twenty-five or more witnesses to say that he was killed by a meteor.

When we reached Lost Lake a little later, the party had settled down to humming and drinking, not necessarily in that order in some cases. From where we hit the lake you cannot see our little cluster of log cabins. All that meets the eye is what looks like an endless expanse of a flat white field. The ice, which was now about three feet thick, lay under five or six feet of snow.

"I wonder why they call it Lost Lake," Paar said. "It's *easy* to find. All you have to do is take Admiral Byrd lessons."

"I think it's lonesome," someone said.

"Yeah," Julie Newmar said, "no neighbors?"

"Sure," I said. "Mr. and Mrs. Trilby—they're eighty years old. They live over there—only about sixty miles from here."

"They sound like fun—maybe we could drop in on them on the way back," Paar said.

"Good idea," said Merv, "I'll take an extra week off."

"Where's the lake?" Miriam Paar said.

"It's right here—in front of you—under the snow."

"Oh," she said, "I wish I had a Hershey bar."

"Hey," yelled the Drunk, "there's a light flashing out there. Somebody's signaling us!"

"Maybe it's a warning," Joey Bishop said. And that's all he said the whole time he was at Lost Lake.

I explained that what they saw was a flasher light which I had set up on four of the islands so we could find our way on moonless nights.

"Tonight is moonless," Tony Randall said, in a moment of pure revelation.

We crossed the ice, from island to island, keeping well spaced out, because although I knew the ice was thick enough to support the weight, I was wary of any air holes which I may have missed in previous crossings.

"I don't hear any wolves," Julie Newmar said. "I love wolves," she added without a trace of innuendo.

"I only promised," I said. "I didn't guarantee."

At that moment, almost as I finished speaking, a wolf howled, and in the still of the winter's night (we had stopped for a moment at island number three), it sounded quite close, but it could have been a mile or so away.

"What was *that*?" Diahann Carroll said in her smallest voice.

"That was a choo-choo train whistle," the Drunk said.

"I love choo-choo train whistles," Julie said.

"Where's the choo-choo train?" Miriam Paar said, practically.

"Can't be more than a hundred miles from here," I said. "You know how sound travels over water."

"Where's the water?" the Drunk said.

"Under you," I said.

The Drunk laughed. "Boy I'm really floatin'," he said.

Everyone had the good taste not to comment.

After we rounded a tree-covered hook of land, we could suddenly see our home island. I had planned our route this way. I wanted it to be like the first rise of the curtain on a spectacularly designed stage set. I wanted the audience to burst into spontaneous delighted applause.

"There it is," I said, with a big lump rapidly forming in my throat. "That's where we live."

There was a long moment of silence, while everyone stared at the indirect multicolored lighting of the majestic pines surrounding the warm yellow-windowed lodge. From where we were, our home island looked like a frozen Garden of Eden, floating on undulating white fleece. The heavy snow on the branches of the pines and the balsams and the hemlocks sparkled marvelous blues, greens, reds, and yellows. It was breathtaking. A murmur of unexpected enchantment crescendoed to cries of unbelieving delight and wonder. Then, from across the purple snows of this never-never land of frozen wilderness and wonder, came the strains of "Auld Lang Syne." Our friends became very quiet. Almost reverent. And when I looked at them and our home and up at the brilliance of the heavens, then out toward the blackness of the thousands of square miles of uninhabited forest, I felt that this was the happiest night of my life. There was another wolf-howl. Very near. This time it was from Tanuki, our wolf.

"That goddamn train is gettin' closer!" the Drunk said.

The party was a huge success. From the cocktails and hors d'oeuvres to the dawn's early light it didn't stop being fun. The Drunk passed out early and we laid him parallel to the polar bear rug. Jake warmed up again and started pinching Diahann Carroll and Miriam Paar—simultaneously. His taste was certainly Catholic, and I admired him for it, but I had to chain him outside for a while before he took off for the moon on his gossamer wings. Dean sang all his old hits and quite a few of his misses. Jack Paar, Johnny Carson, and Merv Griffin played jacks and Joey Bishop kept looking at his watch. I kept looking at Julie Newmar and Diahann Carroll and Reiko.

The piano player, whom I had hired from the Pink Muskrat Motel Lounge in Chinookville, was tireless, which I would consider to be his main weakness, but no one else noticed. At twelve midnight he played what he thought was "Auld Lang Syne" while everybody sang "Tiptoe Through the Tulips," which I will not attempt to explain.

Bobby went to sleep on the floor with his head on the polar bear's and his feet on the Drunk's and looked like a little stoned angel. Reiko, wearing a lovely silk Japanese kimono and mukluks (in case she had to go out and get more firewood), was everywhere. She *never* wants to give a party but seems to enjoy every minute when she does.

There were a few untoward incidents during the lovely evening: I hadn't thought to *brief* our guests, using the one-and-only indoor bathroom, which I should have, because right next to the bathroom—separated by a heavy glass window—

is a former greenhouse, in which we now kept Pussycat, the cougar. Apparently, sitting there, cozily reading *St. Nicholas Magazine*, and then suddenly becoming shockingly aware that a 150-pound cougar was crouching not more than two feet away—staring at you with unblinking, wild, amber eyes— were unsettling to the tranquillity of the moment. These innocents had no way of knowing there was a half inch of plate-glass window between them and what they thought was the end. I don't know what they had planned for their last few moments on earth, but this *definitely* wasn't *it*. Who could play *Camille* sitting on a toilet? John Wayne? Maybe.

Their unearthly shrieks for help revised our powder room setup. Pussycat remained at her advantageous post, but we tacked a BEWARE OF THE COUGAR sign on the bathroom door. This inhibited the beer drinkers, but it was the best we could do on such short notice.

Party guests, we knew, were not all of the same genre when it came to the will to survive, so the weak became separated from the strong at various and inconvenient times during the long night. These tenderlings had to be escorted to their quarters, which might not have been too much of a problem if all the various paths to the well-scattered guest cabins had been cleared. The route to the cabins farthest from the main lodge had not been touched by the fine Italian hand of Jake guiding the fine Sears snowblower and were still some five or six feet below a deep layer of virgin snow. This meant unanticipated trouble. Have you ever tried putting snowshoes on a drunk?

One writer friend, whose career as a New Year's Eve guest had passed its zenith, was extremely tractable when I was fastening the bindings on *his* snowshoes, in preparation for having him retire for the night, which made me suspicious, and I was right. After a tenuous journey through the heaviest of drifts, he decided he was Nelson Eddy and starting singing "Indian Love Call" about as far off-key as I have heard it. Then he said, "Jack, you old sonofabitch, you got the right idea! Get away off in the woods and fuck *everybody*."

"Little hard to do," I said, "if you're way off in the woods."

"You know what I'm gonna do?" he said, after he had fallen flat on his face for the nineteenth time. "I'm gonna stay right here with you and *write*. I'm gonna write wonderful wonderful wonderful novels—of love, and pain . . . and incest and murder and rape and sex and . . . and what *else* is there?"

"Humping," I said.

"Oh, yeah," he said. "Do you think they'll buy that?"

I didn't answer and after a moment he began again on "Indian Love Call," only this time he was Jeanette Mac-Donald.

The party was over. The dawn came in all pink and gold and after a while we hauled all our lovely guests out to meet Toomey Sillins' bus, and as we waved good-bye as the bus curved off into the brilliant sunshine and to the Chinookville Airport, Reiko and Bobby and I stood with our arms around each other in the middle of Route 365. We were very happy on that bright New Year's Day. We had wonderful friends, a new baby, and a grand new life.

"What do you wanna do with *him?*" Jake said, indicating the former Jeanette MacDonald, sleeping peacefully, in back of his snowmobile.

28

THIS is our second winter at Lost Lake, and there's snow and ice and cold and silence and peace. There are long black nights and short brilliant days. Some nights are magic with the wonderfully weird phenomena of the northern lights' "fade-in fade-out" of wild patterns of ever-moving wave after wave of yellow-green luminosity bordered below in red, soaring from the horizon to directly overhead and bursting into fantastic corona, then disappearing behind the jet outlines of the tall pines on the low hills of the far end of the lake. The mood music for this heavenly display was provided by the low moaning howl of Tanuki, Chibi, and our other wolves—echoed mournfully by wild wolves in the far distance.

The northern lights did not appear often enough to make it commonplace. On the other nights we watched television. I should say *I* watched television, which wasn't half so entertaining as the aurora borealis, because as I have said, on the channel we were able to pick up, it seemed like hockey and *The Glenn Miller Story* were self-perpetuating. The score changed in the hockey games, but *The Glenn Miller Story*, as often as I watched it, was never different. Just once, I wanted to see Glenn get on that plane, which he boarded to disappear forever, get hijacked and land in Cuba.

There was another channel we could pick up most of the time, but this featured everything in French, which was amusing, because even a cooking lesson sounded sexy. I tried to learn to speak a little of this charming language by listening to this channel, but picked up exactly nothing. Nothing practical. Never once did anyone say, in French, "I have a red pencil box." "What color is my red pencil box?" "Blue." One night they had *The Glenn Miller Story* on this channel—in French. This was a big night—I thought I had discovered a dirty movie with Jimmy Stewart, which immediately brought to mind wild and wonderful ideas for something new for people over thirty or under sixteen. Think about it! A film with Jimmy Stewart in the nude—chasing a nude Hermione Gingold. And they're both walking. Later. Much later, when he catches up to her it turns out to be Walter Brennan in a Diana Ross wig. And they walk hand in hand into the sunset. Where they meet Rex Harrison and Richard Burton coming back from their honeymoon. Richard is pushing a baby carriage. And Rex is overworking his eye twinkle.

Winter at Lost Lake precludes outdoor sports like swimming and tennis, but there is plenty of other activity. Reiko and Bobby go ice fishing, which involves me, because I have to cut a hole through three or four feet of ice so they can do this. This is not fun. I spend an hour and a half pounding away with something which looks like a Solomon Island headhunter's parsley chopper; then Reiko and Bobby ice-fish for twelve minutes, get cold, and come back inside the house. Sometimes they catch a three-inch smallmouth bass, which they bring in, frozen stiff, to show me.

He's too small, so we have to boil him for twenty minutes to get him warmed up enough to put back in the lake. By this time the hole which I have chopped is frozen solid and has to be chopped anew to allow the unhappy baby bass to go back to its mother. And I'm ready to go back to *my* mother.

Something else we do in the winter is go moose spotting by plane. Charlie Burke flies down in the Cessna 180 and off we go. The moose are easy to spot from the air in the winter because the leaves are off those trees that lose their leaves in winter and the moose are very black against the stark white of the snow. I have reel after reel of rotten movies of moose. They're rotten because moose are very hard to see in the movie—they are not afraid of the plane and just don't move when we fly over. Consequently I have thousands of feet of black blobs in the snow, which I try to convince my audience, when I have one, are immobile moose. This has added greatly to my vast collection of askance looks.

There are two smaller lakes near ours. One is called Moose Lake and the other is Loon Lake. I've never seen a moose at the former or a loon at the latter, but they are nice places to visit with a snowmobile because there is a trail of sorts leading to each. We have two snowmobiles and we use the buddy system when traveling in any remote area, just as scuba divers are supposed to do. This is in case one of the machines breaks down. If this happens, we all can pile on the other and get back to camp. If they *both* break down, we cry. But as buddies.

I can't say enough nice things about these wonderful little vehicles and neither can a very enterprising gentleman around the charming resort area of Timigami. He used one last winter to visit twenty-six bush camps and steal twenty-six racks of moose antlers and twenty-six polar bear rugs, which I told you was the "in" thing in every nothern camp.

This ambitious thief sold these necessaries to twenty-six *other* camp owners, who had been very unhappy until this good fairy roared into their dull, drab, insignificant lives on his Magic Ski-doo.

This icy-nosed Robin Hood was eventually apprehended and is now serving time at the Washburn "Honor Farm," which is the reason we remove the sparkplugs from each of our snowmobiles when we have to leave them unguarded for any length of time.

Snowshoeing is another of our winter pastimes, and I must say here that if for any reason I had to use this method of transportation in case of an emergency, and I had to travel more than a mile—no matter *what* the emergency—I couldn't make it. Better shorten that to a half mile—or less. When you walk with snowshoes, which you must in deep snow or you couldn't move at all, you use muscles that are nonexistent in the human leg. These ethereal strings, after a few moments of lifting one leaden foot past the other in deep snow, start to knot themselves up into tiny knots, which multiply and spread from ankle to crotch and back again, and within a very short time you don't have legs—you have galvanized-iron long johns stuffed with broken glass. The pain is *not* exquisite, unless you're a young masochist and can imagine that you are being deliciously tormented by Sandra Dee—or an old masochist getting the works from Sandra Dee's mother. Or her father if you're a queer old masochist.

But so much for the fun, or Krafft-Ebing side of the picture. "Snowshoe sickness," or *mal de raquette*, as it is known among the Quebec freedom fighters, is a very painful malady. And there is no easy treatment. Only a counter-irritant, which I understand is used by lumberjacks. *Hardy* lumberjacks. When these leg muscles tighten and scream with protest over being called to perform above and beyond, and the pain becomes unbearable, all you have to do is lay a red-hot poker against your leg and immediately the effect is like a mother's lullaby—accompanied by a slight aroma of you, barbecuing.

Winter is like summer in some respects. There are always the same chores, such as filling the gasoline tank which feeds the generators. The gasoline comes in 10-gallon drums, which weigh 85 pounds, and is left at the junction of Route 365 and our timber road every two weeks or so, to be hauled by me and the Jesus-5 back to our camp. It wasn't quite as handy as having the Cozy Oil Company truck back into your driveway, as was the custom back in Old New Litchridge. It was strenuously unhandy. Reiko and I and Bobby had to roll these heavy drums up a plank ramp and into two metal toboggans I had made for this purpose. We would get twenty drums at each delivery, and by the time we got them loaded we weren't too ready for a little game of touch football just to show how carefree and gay we were. Actually, at the conclusion of this necessary task, we were grim. We felt as if we were at the bottom of the good-conduct list at a collective farm in Siberia, because all we could look forward to, after getting the toboggans loaded at the road, was the *unloading* at the camp. It was, we felt each time, as if we were pouring sand down a rat hole, which, incidentally, is a silly custom because the rats eat it.

After we had completed this horrendous biweekly task, we felt good. We felt we were better people for it. We wished better people were *doing* it, but as the Trilbys said, domestic help is very hard to come by 116 miles back in the bush—in the winter.

Another not so gentle task was the changing of the huge metal propane gas bottles. When they were empty, the stove went dead and the empties had to be replaced with fresh, full, immovable bottles. These metal bottles (when full) weighed almost 200 pounds. Empty, they weighed a little less, but not much. And they were not throwaway bottles—we paid a $75 deposit on each bottle and we made goddamn sure they were returned. Ten empties—$750. This is what we got back, but on the other hand when we picked up the ten fresh, full, bottles we had to pay a $750 deposit. The cost of the propane itself was negligible. I think the Chinookville Propane Gas Company is getting rich on the interest they're getting on our deposit money.

Changing these monstrous cylinders required the use of blocks and tackles and ropes and pulleys and muscle and a large profane vocabulary. They were slippery and tricky bastards even in midsummer, but with ice and snow and the cold on their side they became formidable adversaries indeed. On the days we had to wrestle these behemoths around I went to bed early. I didn't give a goddamn about who won the hockey game that night or whether Glenn Miller's trombone lip went bad in reel one or if the Hurons had suddenly gone on the warpath and had us surrounded. I would have surrendered to Maria Tallchief. Or Tonto.

The antenna for our radiotelephone had an annoying habit of blowing off the top of the tall pine tree it was lashed to. An 80-mile-an-hour northern gale had no effect on it, but a gentle, westerly zephyr would send it crashing wildly to earth or suddenly knifing down and embedding itself like a Wilkinson sword blade through our bedroom roof. The first time this happened I was awakened from a sound nightmare and didn't quite know what was going on. My first conclusion was that our bedroom had been stabbed by the Jolly Green Giant, who had revised his thinking on joviality, after seeing *King Kong* on the Late Late Show. Tearing down the Empire State Building, he reasoned, must be a helluva lot more fun than loading little cans of little green peas on little cutie-pie choo-choo trains.

To hoist the radiophone antenna back where it belonged was another camp job that stretched my *profanum vulgus* to its limit. First I had to strap steel spikes to each of my legs and to remember to walk spread-legged so I wouldn't gash myself to death. Anyone viewing me from afar, walking like this and not knowing the situation, might conclude that I was badly in need of a lube job.

Replacing the antenna in the summer was no sinecure, but in the icy cold of a January day I was in danger of becoming the Birdseye quick-frozen tree climber every time I had to do it. I tried those handy pocket warmers to warm my hands, but halfway up the tree I couldn't bend my hands enough to get them in my pockets. And three-quarters of the way up it wouldn't have done any good anyway because my pockets were frozen shut, but inside, my pockets were nice and warm. Which kept the lint from freezing.

In tree climbing, you apparently use the same nonexistent muscles you use for snowshoeing. I discovered this the first time I tried tree climbing, but at the top of the 100-foot pine where the antenna was supposed to be firmly lashed, the view was breathtaking. I could have seen for miles if there hadn't been a blizzard and if the vise-squeezed blood vessels of my legs hadn't spread upwards and tightened my eyeballs.

I tugged on the rope which was the signal to Reiko on the ground to start hauling up the antenna. But nothing like this happened. Every time I tugged on the rope, Reiko tugged back—like we were sending each other messages. Finally I tried an SOS which is three short tugs and three long tugs, then three short tugs again, but after a moment or so, I found that the short tugs and the long tugs were all the same. Besides, how could I spell SOS in Japanese?

Numbed with cold at that altitude, I gave the rope a violent yank and, in turn, was violently yanked back and almost right off the tree. I thought that this might be "Games Japanese People Play—Yank the Yank Out of the Tree," which MacArthur had taught them to bolster their ego and restore their image—and build Toyotas and Datsuns and Hondas. It was so cold, before I became the start of a new totem pole, I decided that unless we reached some common ground on the rope-tugging code, I was wasting my time at the top of that pine, so I climbed down and went into the house to thaw out my hand warmers.

Staying in the house seemed to be the most sensible activity during a northern Ontario winter and that's what we did mostly, but in order to avoid cabin fever, which apparently happens to people when they are cooped up too long in one another's company, we had to devise ways to combat this volatile condition. But first, I don't know why cabin fever is so *localized* and always associated with some *remote* area. I saw more examples of this subtle malady in Old New Litchridge than I've heard of in the bush. Fairfield County in Connecticut is rampant with thousands of married couples who have had cabin fever from about the third year on. Of course, the residents of Westport, Darien, New Canaan, and other Fairfield communities have a ready access to more antidotal remedies than couples who are limited by weather and transportation in the north country.

The cabin-fevered housewife in Fairfield County can always spend her afternoons at the local pub, meeting people who count. And their cabin-fevered husbands can always join a local garden club, which has nightly lectures at the same pub. These outside hobbies may not cure their cabin fever, but if they work it right, they won't bump into each other too often. And sometimes if they *do* accidentally meet at Nick's Nature Study Bar, they may be so looped they'll forget that they are married—to each other—and make arrangements to meet later on at Nick's Nature Study Motel. And so the weekends just fly by.

Our cabin fever is never too much of a problem. We overcome it with love and consideration. This love and consideration reach the shouting stage, occasionally, but who's to hear?

Reiko likes to cook and is forever thinking of new dishes, or I should say new ways to prepare our limited supply of goodies. This occupies quite a lot of her day. The rest of her time is spent in feeding, changing, and burping Timothy—plus trying to get Doggie, the Pomeranian, not to lift his leg on the polar bear's head (his favorite target and he never misses) and defending herself against Pussycat, the cougar, who has a disconcerting habit of springing down on people from the overhead beams. Pussycat does this to me occasionally, but Reiko is her main target—her lovely long hair is much more fun for a cougar. But Pussycat never unsheathes her razor-blade claws, except of course, on the couch, which now resembles paisley shredded wheat. It bleeds a little, too. I've never *seen* such a sensitive couch!

All this keeps Reiko quite busy—patching the couch, patting the baby, and getting her hair back from Pussycat.

Long winter evenings in the bush country are never a problem if you like to read. And I do. I have accumulated, over the years, a tremendously interesting library to which I have been adding since I was a boy. I have everything from *Tom Swift and His Electric Caesarian* to *Tom Swift and His Nuclear Funeral*. It's Tom's whole life in 4,862 well-thumbed volumes. This'll keep you busy on a long winter evening. Unless you're oversexed. I also have, in my library, Bennett Cerf's collection of foreign puns in the original Greek, Yugoslavian, Arabic, and Swahili. This will not only keep you busy but give you many a foreign chuckle. It will also help *make* you oversexed. Or become discouraged with it entirely.

Sometimes when I grow tired of my library, I unlock the large glass case in the living room and fondly examine my large collection of zarfs. I have all kinds. Large zarfs. Small zarfs. Fancy zarfs and plain zarfs. And "zarf" isn't a weird word conjured up by Dr. Seuss to rhyme with some other weird word, also invented by the good doctor. A zarf is a small, metal cuplike stand, richly ornamented, used in the Levant for holding hot coffee cups. And the reason I collect them is that they turn me on. I am also turned on by a small switch under my left armpit which activates a tiny hearing aid which is also a record player and is well stocked with every LP album that Belle Barth ever made. This microscopic device used to be a lifesaver at large cocktail parties. You never heard a word of what anyone was saying to you, but the silly smile on your face never faded.

Many a long winter night we just sit in front of the fireplace—staring at the little orange-colored flames gradually melting the ice out of the white birch logs. We sit silently, reveling in the sweet melancholy of memory. Reiko, remembering her childhood in Japan when the victorious American soldiers brought not pillage and looting, but Pepsi-Cola. Bobby, the flicker of flames lighting his beautiful little face, remembering when he had *children* to play with instead of beavers. Baby Timothy in his crib, close to the fire, remembering his mother's womb, where he was warm all around—instead of scorched on one side and iced up on the other.

As I languish, deliciously relaxed, surrounded by my little family and my dogs, sleeping on the bright-red carpet in front of the hearth, and with our lovely cougar, dozing high up on a beam, with all four legs dangling, the black tip of her long tail below them, twitching endlessly, as she dreams of her lonely Utah mountains, which she has never seen, I am completely at peace with myself and the world.

How did it all work out this way? I wish I knew. I only know that this sudden gift of tranquillity was a long time coming, and mainly because I had been searching for it in the wrong places. Strange as it may sound, the lush, tropical, sun-drenched islands of the South Pacific are not so tranquil as the silent emptiness of the vast reaches of northern Canada.

Charlie Burke, who loves this snowy, unpredictable, contrary northland with a passion usually reserved for something more manageable, put it one way when he got a letter from an old friend who had "deserted" the snow country and had moved to one of those stucco, red-roofed boxes in Fort Lauderdale. This old friend had sent Charlie a snapshot of himself. It showed a tidy sun-splashed garden of lovely roses and a neat white picket fence with Charlie's friend posed in front of it leaning on a lawn mower. On the back of the photo the friend had written "Taken on New Year's Day."

"The poor bastard," Charlie said, "still cutting grass in January."

Keep Up With The BESTSELLERS!